DK EYEWITNESS

T0063868

TOP 10
GOA

Top 10 Goa Highlights

The Top 10 of Everything

CONTENTS

Goa
Area by Area

Streetsmart

Within each Top 10 list in this book, no hierarchy of quality or popularity is implied. All 10 are, in the editor's opinion, of roughly equal merit.

Title page, front cover and spine *Colourful fishing boats on the Baga River*
Back cover, clockwise from top left *Anjuna Flea Market; Anjuna Beach; Maruti Temple, Panaji; Palolem Beach; Velha Goa*

The rapid rate at which the world is changing is constantly keeping the DK Eyewitness team on our toes. While we've worked hard to ensure that this edition of Goa is accurate and up-to-date, we know that opening hours alter, standards shift, prices fluctuate, places close and new ones pop up in their stead. So, if you notice we've got something wrong or left something out, we want to hear about it. Please get in touch at **travelguides@dk.com**

Welcome to
Goa

Idyllic beaches, sleepy fishing villages dotted with pretty white-washed churches, grand Indo-Portuguese mansions, mouthwatering coastal cuisine and lively nightlife heighten Goa's appeal as one of the country's most popular holiday destinations. Whether you're looking for a relaxed beach holiday or a cultural break, this enticing destination will offer you an experience, quite simply, like no other. With DK Eyewitness Top 10 Goa, it's yours to explore.

India's sunshine state has a distinct culture with ample evidence of the 400-odd years of Portuguese rule still apparent in the people's dress, language, cuisine and music. Its capital, **Panaji**, and **Central Goa** are at the historic and cultural heart, home to the Latin-influenced old quarter, **Fontainhas**, **Old Goa's** glorious Baroque churches, the exotic spice plantations of **Ponda**, **Mollem's** wild nature reserves and the spectacular **Dudhsagar Falls**.

Goa's splendid beaches stretch over 105 km (65 miles), drawing around two million visitors every year. From Querim in the north to Polem in the south, each beach has a distinct character. The continuous string of bustling **North Goa** beaches, including **Baga**, **Candolim**, **Calangute** and **Anjuna**, are packed with upscale resorts while Arambol and Mandrem have a bohemian vibe. The serene **South Goa** beaches on the other hand offer a more relaxed atmosphere. A study in contrasts, Goa is simultaneously traditional and modern, noisy and serene.

Whether you're visiting for a weekend or a week, our Top 10 guide brings together the best of everything Goa has to offer, from palm-fringed golden beaches to a vibrant nightlife. The guide has useful tips throughout, from seeking out what's free to avoiding the crowds, plus six easy-to-follow itineraries, designed to tie together a clutch of sights in a short space of time. Add inspiring photography and detailed maps, and you've got the essential pocket-sized travel companion. **Enjoy the book, and enjoy Goa.**

Clockwise from top: Palolem Beach, Church of St Francis of Assisi, colourful Goa Carnival float, paddy field in South Goa, Fort Aguada, Baga Beach shacks, spices at Anjuna Flea Market

Exploring Goa

A favourite year-round holiday destination, Goa is packed with things to see and do. While it is tempting to find the perfect beach and just luxuriate there, the equally enticing hinterland offers an amazing variety of treasures to discover. Whether your visit is short or long, these itineraries will ensure that you experience the very best that Goa has to offer.

Tropical Spice Plantation grows a wide variety of spices and fruits. Spices have long been a principal export and an essential ingredient in Goa's fiery cuisine.

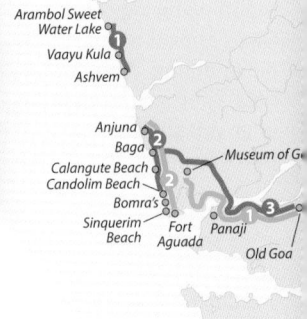

Key
— Two-day itinerary
— Seven-day itinerary

Two Days in Goa

Day ❶
MORNING
Begin with a heritage walk of **Panaji's** (see pp20–23) Latin Quarter, Fontainhas. Next, visit the Church of Our Lady of the Immaculate Conception, the city's most important landmark.
AFTERNOON
Explore the renowned **Basilica de Bom Jesus** (see pp26–7) in **Old Goa** (see pp24–5) before visiting the **Museum of Goa** (see p13) in Pilerne to admire the stunning collection of artworks. In the evening, head back to **Panaji** (see pp20–23) for a cruise along the Mandovi.

Day ❷
MORNING
Head to **Fort Aguada** (see p12), set on a hilltop, to enjoy the superb views. Then take a break to relax at **Sinquerim Beach** (see p12). Stop at **Bomra's** (see p95) for excellent Burmese cuisine.

AFTERNOON
Enjoy windsurfing or parasailing at **Calangute Beach** (see p16). Wander through the bustling **Anjuna Flea Market** (see p12). You can try some Greek cuisine for dinner and enjoy views from **Thalassa** (see p95).

Seven Days in Goa

Day ❶
Start the day early with a yoga session at **Ashvem** (see p18). Enjoy breakfast at **Vaayu Kula's** (see p115) beachfront restaurant, then walk to the **Arambol Sweet Water Lake** for a refreshing dip.

Day ❷
At **Anjuna** (see p15) shop for souvenirs at the famous flea

Agonda Beach is famous as the nesting site for Olive Ridley turtles. Its calm waters that make it a great spot to relax and unwind.

0 kilometres   15

0 miles   15

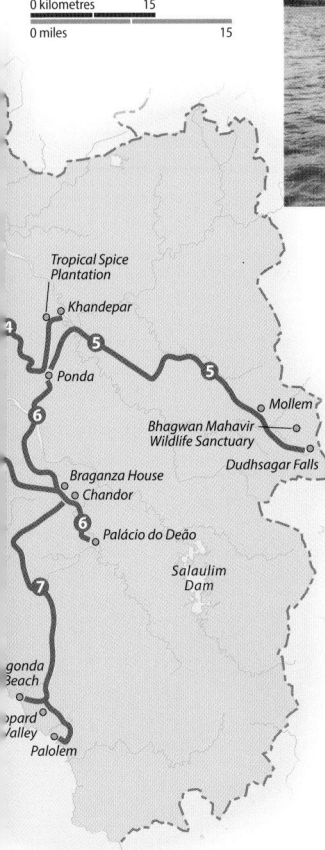

Tropical Spice Plantation

Khandepar

Ponda

Mollem

Bhagwan Mahavir
Wildlife Sanctuary

Dudhsagar Falls

Braganza House

Chandor

Palácio do Deão

Salaulim
Dam

gonda
Beach

opard
Valley

Palolem

market. Next, try your hand at a range of watersports at **Calangute Beach** *(see p16)*. Relax under a parasol on **Candolim Beach** *(see p12)*. Later, enjoy **Baga's** *(see p16)* legendary nightlife.

Day ❸
Visit some of the oldest churches in **Old Goa** *(see pp24–5)*, a UNESCO

World Heritage Site. From here head to **Panaji** *(see pp20–23)* to explore the capital's oldest district, Fontainhas.

Day ❹
Head to **Ponda** *(see pp30–31)* to visit the many temples here. Next, take a tour of the Tropical Spice Plantation and enjoy a Goan buffet lunch. Then, head north to the village of Khandepar to admire the rock-cut caves, one of Goa's oldest historical monuments.

Day ❺
Set out early for the village of **Mollem** *(see pp32–3)*, the main entry point to the Bhagwan Mahavir Wildlife Sanctuary. Explore the sanctuary before heading to Dudhsagar Falls for a swim.

Day ❻
Visit Goa's heritage city, **Margao** *(see pp34–5)*. Take a tour of the grandest colonial mansion in the state, Braganza House. Stop for a traditional meal at the Palácio do Deão. In the evening, head to **Zeebop** *(see p103)* at Utorda Beach for great sunset views.

Day ❼
Start at quiet **Agonda Beach** *(see p38)*, a nesting site for the endangered Olive Ridley turtles. Next, head to Palolem for kayaking. Then make your way to **Leopard Valley** *(see p102)* for a night of dancing.

Top 10 Goa Highlights

Local fishers on a wooden outrigger boat on Baga River

🔟 Goa Highlights

With its tropical setting and idyllic beaches, Goa needs little introduction. India's smallest state, has much more than sublime beaches. It is steeped in history and offers a multitude of cultural experiences, which is what makes it one of the most desirable tourist destinations.

1 Candolim and Around

Upscale Candolim is great for watersports. Its white sands stretch all the way to the 17th-century Fort Aguada *(see pp12–13)*.

2 Vagator, Anjuna and Around

Dramatic hilltops and Chapora Fort provide Vagator Beach with a pretty backdrop. Adjacent Anjuna is famous for its flea market *(see pp14–15)*.

3 Calangute and Baga

Goa's busiest beaches are home to countless shops, hotels, restaurants and nightclubs. The bustling Arpora Saturday Night Bazaar is a highlight *(see pp16–17)*.

4 Ashvem and Around

The quietest stretch on Goa's north coast, Ashvem is popular for its yoga retreat centres and is perfect for watersport activities *(see pp18–19)*.

5 Panaji

Portuguese-inspired architecture, whitewashed churches, the pretty Latin-influenced old quarter along with traditional local cuisine are all found in Goa's relaxed capital, Panaji, overlooking the Mandovi *(see pp20–23)*.

Old Goa

Once the Portuguese capital in India, glorious Old Goa still retains a number of beautiful Baroque churches as well as a magnificent cathedral and a basilica. These are considered to be among Goa's most significant monuments *(see pp24–7)*.

Ponda and Around

The town of Ponda is known for its numerous Hindu temples while its environs are home to exotic spice plantations *(see pp30–31)*.

Mollem and Around

With plenty of forest trails and a variety of bird and plant species, Mollem's lush nature reserves feature a wealth of attractions. It is also home to India's second highest waterfall, Dudhsagar *(see pp32–3)*.

0 km   10
0 miles   10

Valpoi
voi Verem
Khandepar
ol
Ponda
utolim   8 Mollem
Shigao   Colem
Margao   Bhagwan
Mahavir
Wildlife
Sanctuary
Sanguem
Quepem
ncolim   Salaulim
Rivona   Dam
Netravali
Wildlife
Sanctuary
Palolem &
Agonda   Cotigao
Wildlife
Sanctuary

Margao and Around

Scattered around South Goa's main market town Margao are many picturesque villages, which are home to stunning 18th- and 19th-century Goan mansions *(see pp34–7)*.

Palolem, Agonda and Around

Picture-postcard perfect Palolem is known for its sunset views. Neighbouring Agonda and Galgibaga are nesting sites of the Olive Ridley turtles *(see pp38–9)*.

🏆10 ★ Candolim and Around

Once a sleepy fishing village in North Goa, Candolim derives its name from the Konkani word *kandoli* meaning dykes – a reference to the system of sluices used to reclaim the land from the nearby marshes. In 1787, it was at the centre of an attempt made to overthrow the Portuguese. Today, it is famous for its beach, Our Lady of Hope Church and nearby attractions such as Fort Aguada, Reis Magos and the Museum of Goa. A string of bars, restaurants and nightclubs line its main street and side lanes.

1 Fort Aguada
This fort **(above)** was built in 1612 as a defence against the Marathas and the Dutch. Its church is dedicated to St Lawrence, the patron saint of sailors. Some of the buildings in it once housed the state prison.

2 Candolim Beach
South of Calangute, this beach **(below)** stretches all the way to Fort Aguada. Popular with tour groups, the once peaceful waters *(see p89)* now resound with the whir of jet skis and speedboats.

3 Fort Aguada Lighthouses
In the centre of the fort is a four-storey lighthouse, erected in 1864, which is the oldest of its kind in Asia. The new lighthouse, built in 1976, is open to the public and offers great views from the top.

4 Reis Magos Church
Adjacent to the fort is the Reis Magos Church. Constructed in 1555, this is one of Goa's earliest churches, and has the royal Portuguese coat of arms on its façade.

Candolim and Around

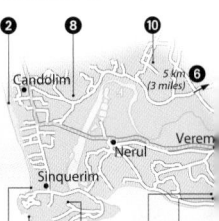

5 Reis Magos Fort
The fort at Reis Magos was built in 1551 by Portuguese viceroy Don Alfonso de Noronha as a line of defence. It once housed a prison. Today, it is a cultural centre with a gallery showcasing Goan artist Mario Miranda's works and an exhibition detailing the history and restoration of the fort.

8 Our Lady of Hope Church

The bell towers of this unique church **(left)**, built in Mannerist Neo-Roman style, rise higher than the central gable. The church has a relic of the blessed Mother Teresa in the form of a drop of blood as well as her statue.

SUBODH KERKAR

Goan artist, Subodh Kerkar, has chronicled Goa's rich history through his work. At the Museum of Goa, look out for an old Goan fishing boat, adorned with antique Chinese soup spoons to highlight the history of the Chinese trade, while the huge chilli sculptures serve as a silent reminder of the old spice route.

10 Museum of Goa (MOG)

Founded by Subodh Kerkar, MOG (Konkani for love) features contemporary art by Indian and international artists. It also has an art store and café (see p90).

6 Houses of Goa Museum

This boat-shaped building (see p90), designed by architect Gerard da Cunha, showcases the history of Goan architecture. Displays are spread across levels interconnected by a spiral staircase.

7 Devil's Finger

This scenic spot, close to Fort Aguada, is the perfect place to enjoy stunning sunset views.

9 Sinquerim Beach

Extending up to the ramparts of Fort Aguada, Sinquerim Beach **(above)** has three luxury hotels on its sands. A few reliable operators offer a range of watersports facilities as well as boat trips.

NEED TO KNOW

Fort Aguada & Fort Aguada Lighthouses: **MAP J6**; Fort Aguada Rd, 0982 359 3995; open 9:30am–6pm daily

Candolim Beach: **MAP H5**

Reis Magos Church: **MAP J6**; Nerul–Reis Margos Rd; 0832 240 2370; open 6am–11pm daily

Reis Magos Fort: **MAP J6**; Verem; open 9:30am–5pm Tue–Sun; www.reismagos fort.com

Houses of Goa Museum: **MAP K5**; H. No. 674, Torda; 0832 241 0711; adm

Devil's Finger: **MAP J6**

Our Lady of Hope Church: **MAP J5**; Candolim; 0832 248 9084; open daily

Museum of Goa (MOG): **MAP J5**; Plot No 79, Pilerne Industrial Estate, Pilerne; open 10am–6pm daily; adm; www.museumofgoa.com

Sinquerim Beach: **MAP H6**

■ Take an evening ferry from Panaji to the Fort Aguada Jail complex, and arrive just in time to enjoy the sunset.

TOP 10 ⭐ Vagator, Anjuna and Around

A beautiful bay sheltered by rocky outcrops at both ends, Vagator consists of a number of small beaches fringed by shady coconut palms. Looming above it are the red laterite ruins of Chapora Fort. Neighbouring Anjuna, known for its laidback vibe and the sprawling weekly flea market, has been a popular destination since the 1960s. Nearby are the pretty villages of Assagao, Siolim and North Goa's largest town, Mapusa.

3 Goa Collective Bazaar

Every Friday, HillTop (see p56) transforms into one big night bazaar (see p62), with colourful stalls selling clothing, jewellery, drinks, food, souvenirs and much more. There's live music too.

YOGA RETREATS IN NORTH GOA

Goa is the perfect place to immerse yourself in a yoga retreat. Inland from Anjuna, Assagao is the heartland of yoga with numerous retreats (see p92). Some of them even run training programmes for teachers. The Himalaya Yoga Valley, the Satsanga Retreat and the Purple Valley Centre are among the most popular ones in North Goa.

1 Chapora Fort

Now in ruins, this fort (above) was built by the Portuguese in 1717 on the remains of a bastion erected by Adil Shah. Its name is derived from "Shahpura", or "Town of the Shah", as the village was once known. The ramparts offer great coast views.

Vagator, Anjuna and Around

2 Vagator Beach

Scenic Vagator's main beach (see p46) is known as Big Vagator (below). To the south is secluded Little (or Ozran) Vagator where the main attraction is the face of Lord Shiva, carved out of the rocks.

4 Anjuna Beach

With its calm waters and palm trees, Anjuna *(see p89)* is one of the most scenic beaches of North Goa. A haven for backpackers, it is known for its rave parties.

5 Anjuna Flea Market

This popular Wednesday flea market **(below)** sells everything from Balinese batik and papier-mâché boxes to Tibetan prayer wheels and handmade leather sandals.

7 Mascarenhas Mansion

Built in the 16th century, this mansion in Assagao has beautiful *balcãos* (balconies) and stained-glass windows with floral designs. On the front porch there is an L-shaped wooden seat.

8 Mapusa

The highlight here is the lively Friday market *(see p63)*, with its tantalizing aromas of dried fish, spices and the spicy Goan sausages, *chouriço*. In demand are the region's famous cashew nuts.

10 Siolim

Set amid pretty verdant surroundings, the riverside town of Siolim *(see p91)* features striking colonial-era houses and the Church of St Anthony **(above)**, believed to be the site of two miracles in the 16th-century.

6 Assagao

Beautiful Assagao *(see pp90–91)* is full of Indo-Portuguese houses, a number of which have been restored to their former glory and transformed into chic cafés, restaurants and shops.

9 Omaggio Goa

This unique performing arts studio is great for learning gymnastics, aerial circus, acrobatics and various dance forms. It offers classes for both kids and adults.

NEED TO KNOW

Chapora Fort: **MAP H3**; Chapora Fort Rd, Chapora; 0832 249 4200

Vagator Beach & Anjuna Beach: **MAP H4**

Goa Collective Bazaar: **MAP H4**; Ozran Beach Rd, Vagator; open Nov–Apr: 3pm–3am Fri

Anjuna Flea Market: **MAP H4**; Anjuna Beach; open Nov–Apr: 8am–sunset Wed

Assagao: **MAP J4**

Mascarenhas Mansion: **MAP J4**; Assagao

Mapusa: **MAP J4**; open 8am–6:30pm daily

Omaggio Goa: **MAP H4**; Anjuna–Calangute Rd, Anjuna; 8691 850 104

Siolim: **MAP J3**

■ The Assagao Mehfil (09545718824) hosts music concerts and dance performances at Mojigao's *(see p92)* lovely café.

■ Enjoy a bird watching tour with Rahul Alvarez (www.rahulalvares.com).

TOP 10 ⭐ Calangute and Baga

The centre of the hippie scene in the 1960s and 1970s, Calangute is Goa's most crowded beach. During the day, it is packed with sunbathers, trinket stalls and hawkers. The entire stretch of sand is lined with bars and restaurant beach shacks that serve Goan food. En route to the neighbouring picturesque village of Saligao is the colonial Casa dos Proença mansion and the churches of Mae de Deus and St Alex. Extending north of Calangute, Baga Beach is far less crowded, although its expanse of soft, white sand has its share of guesthouses and late-night clubs and bars along Tito's Lane.

Calangute Beach

Once regarded as the "queen of beaches", this is Goa's busiest beach (see p89). There's plenty for visitors to explore here including the market town, which has several Kashmiri-run handicraft boutiques and Tibetan stalls selling crafts and miniature paintings.

NEED TO KNOW

Baga Beach & Calangute Beach: **MAP H5**

Mario Gallery: **MAP H5**; Pedru Martina, Calangute; 0744 736 5372

Mae de Deus Church: **MAP J5**; Chogm Rd, Saligao; 0832 227 8246; open 9am–5pm daily

Tibetan Market: **MAP H5**; Calangute–Baga Rd, Baga; open 11am–11pm daily

St Alex Church: **MAP J5**; near Don Bosco School, Bardez; 0982 359 3995; open 9am–8:30pm daily

Goa Brewing Co. (GBC): **MAP J5**; Chogm Rd, Sangolda; 0832 240 9350

Casa dos Proença: **MAP H5**; Calangute–Baga Rd

Literati: **MAP H5**; E/1-282 Gaura Vaddo, Calangute; 0832 227 7740

② Baga Beach

Next to Calangute, Baga **(above)** is Goa's most developed beach (see p89). It is dotted with several shacks, trendy eateries and lively night spots. Many operators here offer a wide range of thrilling water-sport activities.

③ Mario Gallery

Legendary artist Mario Miranda's (1926–2011) original artworks are on display here. Large and small-size prints of his illustrations and merchandise can be purchased from the store. Miranda was famous for his sketches and cartoons of local characters and Goan culture.

④ Mae de Deus Church

This church **(below)** in Saligao is one of the best examples of Neo-Gothic architecture in Goa. Near the altar is the miraculous statue of Mae de Deus (Mother of God). The church looks stunning when it is illuminated in the evening.

6 Tito's Statue

In 1971, Tito Henry de Souza opened a small eatery to promote tourism in Goa. Today, Club Tito's *(see p56)* is a Goan institution. A life-size statue of Tito **(left)** is located in Baga.

7 Tibetan Market

This market has handcrafted jewellery, clothing and display pieces from Nepal and Tibet. Though expensive, the *objets d'art* leave no room for doubt as to their authenticity.

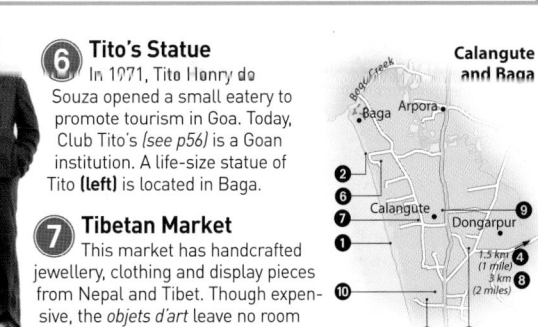

Calangute and Baga

5 St Alex Church

One of the oldest churches in Goa, St Alex's striking façade is dominated by a dome, flanked on each side by bell towers – one has a church bell while the other has a statue of Our Lady. The Rococo-style interior has an ornate pulpit and gilded *reredos*.

9 Casa dos Proença

This grand 18th-century mansion has a distinctive tower-shaped verandah with oyster-shell screens and a unique natural cooling system.

SALIGAO VILLAGE

The tiny village of Saligao, close to Calangute, is a hidden gem waiting to be discovered. Its original name was Salgaon. This was modified by the Portuguese to Saligao – *Sal* meaning wooded forest and *gao* meaning village. The village has many Goan restaurants and beautifully preserved Portuguese houses. Make It Happen Goa *(www.makeithappen.com)* has fantastic walking tours, which take you to popular sights around the village.

8 Goa Brewing Co. (GBC)

This craft brewery is housed in a 250-year-old Indo-Portuguese house. On some Saturdays, it opens its doors to beer lovers who can take a tour and sample favourites like the freshly brewed Eight Finger Eddie.

10 Literati

Set in a 100-year-old Portuguese house, Literati **(below)** has a great collection of books. It hosts literary and cultural events. Visitors can enjoy reading in the Italian-style garden café.

TOP 10 ★ Ashvem and Around

The pristine beaches to the far north of Goa are some of the region's loveliest and are a popular option for many travellers. Yoga, meditation and watersports are ubiquitous here. The beaches of Mandrem and Morjim are perfect for leisurely dips in the ocean. At sunset Ashvem comes alive attracting crowds to its bustling nightlife. Eclectic Arambol (or Harmal), a hippie haven in the 1960s, still retains some of its bohemian vibe.

Ashvem Beach ①

Even though the golden white sands of Ashvem **(right)** are getting crowded with each passing year, its seemingly never-ending shores *(see p46)* still remain the best place to relax under an umbrella.

② Mandrem Beach

The clear blue waters of Mandrem *(see p47)* and its pristine beach offer a peaceful respite from the packed beaches of the north.

④ Surfing in Morjim

Morjim has several places where you can learn to surf **(below)**. The best time for surfing is during the dry winter months from October to April. The Octopus Surf Goa *(see p54)* offers surf board rentals.

⑤ Arambol Beach

Popular Arambol *(see p46)* still has all the charm of a traditional fishing village. Surrounded by low cliffs and featuring several dramatic rocky outcrops that jut into the sea, its calm waters are safe for swimming.

③ Ashiyana Yoga Centre

Set amid tropical gardens **(above)**, this retreat on the banks of the Mandrem River has five yoga *shalas* (studios). It offers world-class yoga classes with accommodation in treehouses and wooden eco-lodges.

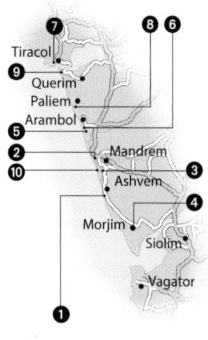

YASHWANTGAD FORT

Near the Maharashtra-Goa border is the 16th-century Yashwantgad Fort (also known as Redi Fort). Take a short drive from Arambol to see the ruins of this tree-entangled fort, built to protect the Konkan from attacks via the coastal route. Just below the fort ruins is Redi beach. The fort is well worth a visit, ideally early in the morning or at dusk.

8 Paliem Sweet Water Lake

At the northern end of Arambol, a rocky footpath leads to a second beach, Paliem, entirely surrounded by cliffs. This sandy cove has a freshwater lagoon **(above)** fed by hot springs and lined with sulphurous mud.

Ashvem and Around

9 Querim Beach

A 5-km- (3-mile-) long path, heading north from Arambol, leads to the quiet Querim Beach (pronounced "keri"). This pristine strip of white sand (see p47) is the perfect place to unwind or simply enjoy a leisurely swim.

10 Kitesurfing, Mandrem

The calm waters of Mandrem are safe for learning kitesurfing. Due to the wind patterns, the kiting season usually begins only in January. Several schools offer beginner and advanced level courses.

6 Paragliding, Arambol

The cliffside near Paliem Sweet Water Lake is a good vantage point for paragliding. For details, check with Arambol Hammocks or the Western India Paragliding Association shack, which is close to the lake.

7 Fort Tiracol

At the northern tip of Goa, this fort (see p71), built by the Marathas in the 17th-century and captured by the Portuguese in the mid-18th century, is now a heritage hotel (see p117). There's a small church inside.

NEED TO KNOW

Ashvem Beach: **MAP G3**

Mandrem Beach: **MAP G2**

Ashiyana Yoga Centre: **MAP G2**; Junas Waddo, Mandrem; 0985 040 1714; open 8am–8pm daily

Octopus Surf Goa: **MAP H3**; Silver Sand Beach Shack and Bamboo Huts, Morjim; 0750 780 8400

Arambol Beach: **MAP G2**

Paragliding, Arambol: Arambol Hammocks;

0961 917 5722; www.arambol.com

Fort Tiracol: **MAP G1**

Paliem Sweet Water Lake: **MAP G2**

Querim Beach: **MAP G1**

Kitesurfing, Mandrem: Kiteguru Kitesurf School; Riverside Hotel, Mandrem; 9371 414 764 open Nov–Mar; www.kiteguru.co.uk

■ Vaayu Kula (see p115) in Mandrem has a lovely art gallery and a restaurant.

🔟⭐ Panaji

Reminiscent of a provincial Mediterranean town, Goa's capital, Panaji is situated at the mouth of the Mandovi River. Formerly a port of the kings of Bijapur, it became a military landing stage after the arrival of the Portuguese in 1510. In 1843, Panaji, or Panjim as it was then called, became the official capital of Portuguese territories in India. Today, it has a relaxed and friendly ambience, notably along the leafy avenues of the old town.

Church of Our Lady of the Immaculate Conception ①
Panaji's most important landmark, this church (**right**), built in 1541, is where Portuguese sailors would come to pray after their long voyage from Lisbon. Its most striking feature is the double flight of stairs leading up to the church (see p75).

② Fontainhas
The narrow winding streets of the city's Latin-influenced old quarter (see p76) is lined with colourful houses, reminiscent of the Portuguese legacy.

③ Statue of Abbé de Faria
This arresting statue (**above**) is a tribute to Goan priest, Abbé de Faria. Born in Candolim, he won acclaim as the father of modern hypnosis. He also finds mention in Alexander Dumas's famous novel, *The Count of Monte Cristo*.

⑤ Ashokan Pillar
In the centre of the Municipal Gardens stands the Ashokan Pillar. The pillar initially featured a bust of explorer Vasco da Gama, but this was later replaced with the Buddhist Wheel of Law or the Ashoka Chakra, India's national emblem.

RIVER CRUISES
A great way to spend an evening in Goa is to take a sunset cruise along the Mandovi River. Some operators (www.konkan explorers.com) offer eco-friendly alternatives to standard river cruises, which help visitors to learn about the culture and heritage of the river Mandovi and Panaji. The starting point for these is from Santa Monica jetty.

④ Gallery Gitanjali
Housed in a heritage complex, this gallery (**below**) is an art and cultural hub. Abstract art is on display here and in Panjim People's, Panjim Inn and Panjim Pousada hotels, which are part of the complex.

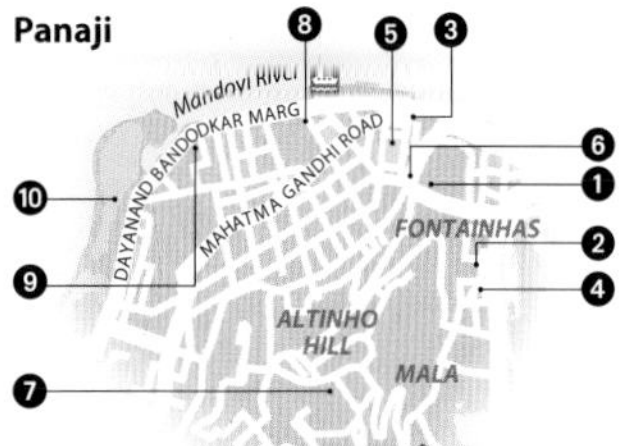

Panaji

8 **Institute Menezes Braganza**

The *azulejos* (blue-and-white painted ceramic tiles) here are the highlight. These depict scenes from the epic *Os Lusiadas*, which recounts the history of the Portuguese presence in Goa.

9 **Palace of Maquinezes**

A great example of Goan period architecture, this building belonged to Portuguese land-owners called Maquinezes.

6 **Church Square**

At the heart of Panaji is a leafy park known as Church Square or the Municipal Gardens, originally named after 16th-century physician, Jardim de Garcia da Orta.

7 **Altinho Hill**

On the eastern edge of Panaji is the hilltop residential district of Altinho, which is home to the Bishop's Palace. The pope stayed at the palace during his visit in 1999.

NEED TO KNOW

Church of Our Lady of the Immaculate Conception: **MAP L2**; Rua Emidio Garcia; open 9am–7:30pm daily

Fontainhas: **MAP L2–M2**

Statue of Abbé de Faria: **MAP L1**

Gallery Gitanjali: **MAP M2**; E-212, 31st January Rd, Fontainhas; 0832 242 3331; open 9am–6pm daily

Ashokan Pillar: **MAP L1**

Church Square: **MAP L1**

Altinho Hill: **MAP L2**; Bishop's Palace: open 9am–5pm Mon–Fri (to 1pm Sat)

Institute Menezes Braganza: **MAP L1**; 0832 222 4143; open 10am–5:30pm Mon–Sat

Palace of Maquinezes: **MAP K1**; Dayanand Bandodkar Marg, Old GMC Complex; 0832 242 8111

Campal Gardens: **MAP K1**

10 **Campal Gardens**

These pleasant riverside gardens **(above)** are a good place to unwind. Visitors can also enjoy paddleboat rides on the Mandovi. Look out for a huge statue of Bhagwan Mahavir (the 24th Jain Tirthankara) here.

Exploring Panaji

Picturesque setting of Cabo Raj Niwas, the oldest residence in the country

1 Cabo Raj Niwas
MAP C3 ■ Raj Bhavan Rd, Dona Paula ■ 0832 245 3506

Constructed in 1540, this fortress (see p76) is the official residence of the Governor of Goa. Inside there's a beautiful 500-year-old chapel.

2 Azad Maidan
MAP L1 ■ MG Rd, near Police Headquarters, Ozari

This grassy square has a pavilion, made using Corinthian pillars taken from a Dominican church. Inside is a memorial to freedom fighter, Dr Tristao de Braganza Cunha.

3 St Sebastian's Chapel
MAP M2 ■ St Sebastian Rd, Altinho

The chapel has a life-size unusual crucifix, which shows Christ with his eyes open. It is believed this was done to inspire fear in those being interrogated during the Inquisition.

Exploring Panaji

4 Old Secretariat
MAP L1 ■ Ave Dom João Castro

This riverfront edifice is one of Panaji's oldest buildings. Originally the summer palace of 16th-century ruler, Yusuf Adil Shah, it was later converted by the Portuguese as a residence for the viceroy. Today, it houses municipal offices and is one of the main venues for the annual Serendipity Arts Festival (see p69).

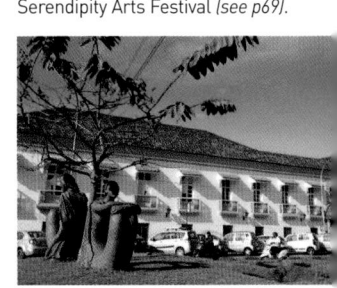

Colonial façade of the Old Secretariat

5 Casa da Moeda
MAP M1 ■ Near Head Post Office ■ www.casadamoedagoa. wordpress.com

In the midst of Panaji's Post Office Square stands the Casa da Moeda (House of Coins). This building served as the Mint of Goa from 1834 to 1841. Guests can enjoy afternoon tea here and learn more about the local history, but before visiting a booking needs to be made at least 48 hours in advance.

6 Public Astronomical Observatory (PAO)

MAP L2 ▪ Junta House, Swami Vivekanand Rd ▪ 0832 222 5726

Located on the terrace of the Junta building, the PAO is the perfect place for astronomy enthusiasts and for those who would like to enjoy great night views of the capital city.

7 Kala Academy

MAP K2 ▪ Dayanand Bandodkar Marg ▪ 0832 242 0452

On the banks of the Mandovi is Goa's main cultural centre, which hosts performing arts events all year round. Built by architect Charles Correa, the complex has an indoor and open-air auditorium, a black box theatre, an art gallery and an on-site café.

8 Pilar Museum

MAP C3 ▪ 12 km (7 miles) SE of Panaji ▪ 0832 221 8521

Set on a hilltop, Pilar Seminary was originally built by the Capuchins (a Franciscan order) in 1613, on the site of an old Hindu temple. It has a small museum, which displays Portuguese coins and a stone lion, the symbol of the Kadamba dynasty.

Roger Ballen's show at Sunaparanta

9 Sunaparanta, Goa Centre for the Arts

MAP L2 ▪ 63/C-8, near Army House, Altinho ▪ www.sgcfa.org

Housed in a pretty villa, Sunaparanta (Konkani for Golden Goa) is a non-profit arts foundation set up by Dipti and Dattaraj Salgaocar. It hosts various events, and has the lovely Café Bodega (see p79).

10 Mangrove Boardwalk

MAP M2 ▪ Near Goa State Museum, Panaji

A wooden walkway built over a mangrove forest, this elevated platform provides a unique opportunity for visitors to explore and admire the beauty of Goa's rich mangrove ecosystem up close.

FONTAINHAS AND SÃO TOMÉ

Tucked away between Ourem Creek and Altinho Hill in Panaji are the old residential quarters of Fontainhas and São Tomé, built on reclaimed land in the 19th century. Fontainhas was named after the fountain of Phoenix, a spring that was the quarter's only source of water. Most of the houses are painted yellow, ochre, green or indigo in keeping with the traditional Portuguese building code that every building, except churches, should be colour-washed after the monsoons. São Tomé takes its name from the tiny church, built in 1849. This old-world precinct, characterized by painted, tile-roofed houses, has streets lined with taverns offering Goan cuisine and *feni* (cashew nut liqueur), and bakeries serving *bebinca*, the delicious local cake.

Rua de Ourem facing Ourem Creek

🔟 ⭐ Old Goa

A magnificent complex of churches spread along a 1.5-km (1-mile) stretch marks the site of Old Goa, the Portuguese capital until the mid-18th century. Portugal's Goa Dourada ("Golden Goa") was once a city inhabited by more than 30,000 people. The area, now a UNESCO World Heritage Site, has two of the state's most important religious monuments, the Basilica de Bom Jesus and the grand Sé Cathedral.

5 Archaeological Museum

Housed in the Convent of St Francis of Assisi, this museum (below) exhibits pre-colonial sculptures. A statue of the Portuguese general, Alfonso de Albuquerque, who conquered Goa in 1510, stands near the museum entrance.

1 Viceroy's Arch

Over 1,000 ships a year brought new arrivals to Goa in the 17th century. They passed under this archway (above), built by Francisco da Gama (Viceroy, 1597–1600).

2 Basilica de Bom Jesus

The basilica (see pp26–7) was the first in South Asia to be granted the status of Minor Basilica in 1946. It is revered by Roman Catholics since it houses the mortal remains of Goa's patron saint, Francis Xavier.

3 Church of St Francis of Assisi

This is one of Old Goa's most important churches (see p45). Built by the Franciscan friars in 1521, it has a carved and gilded main altar, which depicts the crucified Jesus, four Evangelists, St Francis, and Our Lady with the infant Jesus.

4 Church and Monastery of St Augustine

Erected by the Augustinian order in 1597, this Gothic-style church (see p44) was abandoned in 1835, and its roof caved in seven years later. The belfry (below) is all that remains of what was once India's largest church.

7 Church of Our Lady of the Rosary

This is one of Goa's earliest Manueline-style churches. The tomb of Dona Catarina, the first Portuguese woman to migrate to Goa, lies here.

8 Gateway of Adil Shah's Palace

The gate, comprising a lintel and basalt pillars, is all that survives of Yusuf Adil Shah's palace. It was also used as the viceroys' residence until 1695.

THE ARCHITECTURE OF OLD GOA

Most of the buildings encompass a range of European styles, from sober Renaissance to exuberant Baroque and Portuguese Manueline, named after its patron King Manuel I, which uses nautical motifs. Almost all the churches are made of local laterite, a red and porous stone traditionally coated with lime whitewash to prevent erosion during the monsoons.

6 Church of St Cajetan

Built by Italian friars, this church (above) is known for the exuberant wood-carvings on its high altar and pulpit. The dome is laid out in the shape of a Greek cross (see p44).

Old Goa

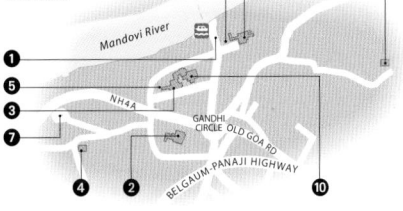

9 Church of Our Lady of the Mount

Goa's first viceroy, Alfonso de Albuquerque, built this church in 1526 after his victory over Yusuf Adil Shah. The church sits on top of a hill and offers great views of Old Goa.

10 Sé Cathedral

Designed in the 16th century and built over a period of 80 years, this cathedral (see p75) is believed to be Asia's largest. The gilded high altar depicts the life of St Catherine of Alexandria on six panels.

NEED TO KNOW

Viceroy's Arch: **MAP M6**

Basilica de Bom Jesus: **MAP M6**; Rua das Naus de Ormuz; 0832 228 5790; open daily

Church of St Francis of Assisi: **MAP M6**; Off NH 4; open 7:30am–6:30pm daily

Church and Monastery of St Augustine: **MAP M6**

Archaeological Museum: **MAP M6**; Convent of St Francis of Assisi;

0832 228 5333; open 9am–5pm Sat–Wed

Church of St Catejan: **MAP M6**; E of Viceroy's Arch; open daily

Church of Our Lady of the Rosary: **MAP M6**

Gateway of Adil Shah's Palace: **MAP M6**

Church of Our Lady of the Mount: **MAP M6**

Sé Cathedral: **MAP M6**; Senate Square; open 7am–6:30pm daily

Basilica de Bom Jesus

Imposing façade of Basilica de Bom Jesus

is mounted on a plinth. At the base are bronze plaques depicting scenes from his life.

1 Façade
This is the only Goan church not covered in lime plaster. The Baroque structure blends Doric, Corinthian, Ionic and composite styles in its three-tiered façade. At the top on a quadrangular pediment is an intricately carved basalt stone tablet, which features the Jesuit motto, IHS or *Iaeus Hominum Salvator*, meaning "Jesus the Saviour" in Greek.

2 Chapel of St Francis Xavier
Inside the basilica is a chapel where the relics of St Francis Xavier are kept. The interior of this chapel has paintings, depicting scenes from the life of the saint.

3 Tomb of St Francis Xavier
The marble-and-jasper three-tiered tomb of St Francis Xavier features the altars, the Florentine mausoleum and the silver casket. In 1698, St Francis's body was moved here on the request of the Duke of Tuscany, Cosimo III, who donated the elaborate tomb in exchange for the pillow that lay under the saint's head. The silver casket containing the saint's body

4 Reredos
One of the highlights is the massive ornate gilded *reredos* (ornamental screen), which extends from floor to ceiling behind the altar. It features spiralling scrollwork, exquisitely carved panels, statues and pilasters.

5 Sacristy
Adjoining the Chapel of St Francis Xavier is a corridor, which leads to the sacristy, accessed by a beautifully carved wooden door. Inside is an altar, that has an iron chest containing the Golden Rose, gifted by Pope Pius XII in 1953.

6 Main Altar
The massive gilt altarpiece is dominated by a statue of St Ignatius of Loyola, founder of the Jesuit Order accompanied by the Infant Jesus (Bom Jesus). The saint is seen gazing above his head at the gilded

The magnificent main altar

sun, which bears the Jesuit emblem IHS. Above this is a depiction of the Holy Trinity.

7 Gallery of Modern Art

On the upper floor of the basilica is a church art gallery, which displays the works of Goan surrealist painter, Dom Martin. The paintings,

which date from 1973 and 1976 depict various Biblical scenes.

8 Interior Courtyard

The courtyard inside has a small garden. From here a corridor leads visitors to the sound and light show, which tells the story of St Francis Xavier.

9 Professed House of the Jesuits

Next to the basilica is a two-storey laterite building, which predates the basilica, having been completed in 1585. The building was used as the priests' quarters until it was damaged by a fire in 1633.

10 Our Lady to Bernadette at Lourdes

Outside there is a grotto with a spring of water, which depicts the apparition of Our Lady to Bernadette at Lourdes.

Paintings at the Gallery of Modern Art

ST FRANCIS XAVIER (1506–1552)

Francis Xavier was sent to Goa by the Portuguese king, Dom Joao III. He arrived in May 1542, aged 36, and worked tirelessly as a missionary over the next few years. He died while on voyage off the coast of China in 1552, and was temporarily buried on an island. When his body was dug up three months later to transfer his bones, it showed no signs of decay. A year later, when his remains were enshrined in the basilica in Goa, his body was still in pristine condition. This was declared a miracle, and in 1622 he was canonized. Expositions of his relics take place every ten years or so; the next one will be in 2024.

Casket with the body of St Francis Xavier

🔟 ⭐ Ponda and Around

A busy commercial centre, Ponda lends its name to the *taluka* (sub-district) of the same name, which is renowned for its 17th- and 18th-century Hindu temples, tucked away in thick forests and the Safa Shahouri Masjid. To the north of the town is a butterfly sanctuary, with over 100 species while to the northeast, near the village of Khandepar, is a cluster of rock-cut caves. In and around Ponda, there are many farms that grow numerous aromatic spices.

1 Naguesh Temple

Built for the worship of Nagesh (Shiva as Lord of the Serpents), this is one of the oldest temples (**above**) in the region. The entrance hall has carved wooden friezes depicting scenes from the epics *Ramayana* and *Mahabharata* (see p45).

SPICE PLANTATIONS

The temple town of Ponda is the centre of spice farms (see p55), known for growing aromatic spices such as cardamom, nutmeg, cinnamon and vanilla, in addition to crops such as cashew, betel nut and coconut. Visitors can learn how the spices are grown by taking a guided tour of the plantation. The tour usually involves a stroll through the orchards and includes a traditional banana-leaf buffet lunch.

---

2 St Roque Chapel

Located atop a hill in Bandoda village, this chapel was built in 1904. The bell, which hangs in the chapel, has inscriptions in Devanagari as well as Portuguese.

3 Tropical Spice Plantation

Visitors will need to cross a bamboo bridge to get to this spice farm (**right**). Bird watchers will enjoy spotting different species when paddle boating around the lake. There's a butterfly garden here (see p84) too.

4 Mystic Woods

This tranquil park, to the north of Ponda (see p83), is filled with colourful seasonal butterflies. It is the perfect spot for a quiet walk. A butterfly conservation project, it features beautiful forest walkways, abundant flora, a spice farm and even a breakfast-with-butterflies tour.

Previous pages Aerial view of the lovely Reis Magos Church

5 Mahalasa Temple

Dedicated to Vishnu, the main deity here was taken from Verna, a village in Salcete. Highlights include a 21-tier brass pillar, rising from a figure of Kurma (Vishnu's incarnation as a turtle), with Garuda, (half man, half eagle) his vehicle, perched on top.

6 Safa Shahouri Masjid

This mosque (above) was built by Ibrahim Adil Shah (successor of Yusuf Adil Shah) in 1560. A ritual tank here (see p84) has the same designs as those on the *mihrabs* (arched niches) inside the mosque.

10 Ponda Fort

Destroyed by the Portuguese in 1549, this fort was rebuilt in 1675 when the 17th-century Maratha leader, Shivaji, conquered the region. Inside, there's a statue in honour of Shivaji.

7 Caves of Khandepar

Deep in the forest, there are four Hindu rock-cut caves (right) from the 10th–13th centuries, with carved lotus decorations on the ceiling, simple door frames and niches for oil lamps.

Ponda and Around

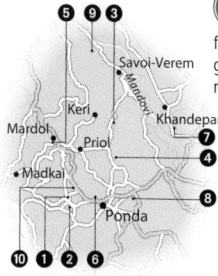

8 Sahakari Spice Farm

This farm is known for adopting organic farming methods for cultivation. It specializes in growing vanilla, spices, cashew nuts, fruits and many different ayurvedic medicinal herbs.

9 Savoi Spice Plantation

About 13 km (8 miles) north of Ponda, is the 200-year-old Savoi Spice Plantation. One of the oldest plantations in Goa, it is known for growing coconuts, betel nuts and spices. There are two fully-equipped village-style huts available for visitors to stay overnight.

NEED TO KNOW

Naguesh Temple: MAP D3; Donshiwado; open 6:30am–12:45pm, 4:30–8:30pm daily

St Roque Chapel: MAP D3; Donshiwado, Bandoda

Tropical Spice Plantation: MAP D3; Arla Bazar, Keri; 0832 234 0329; open 10am–4pm daily; adm

Mystic Woods: MAP D3; Ponda, Priol; 9975 592 347; open 9am–5pm Tue–Sun; adm

Mahalasa Temple: MAP D3; Mahalasa Saunsthan, Mardol; open 6:30am–8:30pm Mon–Fri

Safa Shahouri Masjid: MAP D3; Shahpur Rd, Ponda; open 5am–9pm daily

Sahakari Spice Farm: MAP D3; Ponda Belgaum Highway, Curti; adm

Caves of Khandepar: MAP D3; Deulwada, Surla

Savoi Spice Plantation: MAP D3; 50 Savoi, Marcel Ponda Rd; 0832 231 2394; open 9:30am–4:30pm daily; adm

Ponda Fort: MAP D3; NH 4A, Donshiwado, Bandoda

 Mollem and Around

Close to the Karnataka border, the village of Mollem is the starting point for a region of great natural beauty, abundant wildlife and sacred architectural gems. Bhagwan Mahavir Wildlife Sanctuary is one of the largest protected wildlife areas in Goa. In the southeast corner of the sanctuary is the famous Dudhsagar Falls. The medieval Tambdi Surla temple lies at the northern end, on the dense lower slopes of the Western Ghats.

Dudhsagar Falls **1**

Goa's 600-m- (1,969-ft-) high waterfall **(right)** gets its name Dudhsagar (meaning "sea of milk" in Konkani) from the clouds of white mist that rise when the water level is at its highest. It is best visited after the monsoon from October until December *(see p81)*.

2 Mahishasura Mardini Temple

Dedicated to goddess Navdurga, this temple is believed to be more than 500 years old. The main deity worshipped here is Mahishasura Mardini, a fierce incarnation of goddess Durga created to slay the buffalo-demon, Mahishasura.

3 Bhagwan Mahavir Wildlife Sanctuary and Mollem National Park

One of Goa's most interesting nature reserves, Bhagwan Mahavir Wildlife Sanctuary covers a vast area of 240 sq km (93 sq miles) that also includes Mollem National Park. It is home to jungle cats, deer, leopards **(left)** and *gaurs* (Indian bison) and over 120 bird species. There are several unmarked forest trails here. Guided tours of the park are available.

4 Backwoods Camp

Nature lovers will enjoy a trip to this camp, near Tambdi Surla, which is home to over 170 species of endemic and migratory birds, from the pretty Ceylon frogmouths and Asian fairy bluebirds to the Malabar trogon and Indian pitta. Farmhouse rooms, bungalows and tents are available for stay here.

5 Tambdi Surla Mahadev Temple

This is the oldest existing Hindu temple **(above)** in Goa from the Kadamba period. Dedicated to Shiva, the temple *(see p82)* is built from black basalt and probably survived because of its remote location.

6 Sunset Point

A picturesque spot, which offers lovely views of the tropical evergreen forest. Visitors can hire a four-wheel-drive vehicle at the Mollem check-point to reach here.

Mollem and Around

9 Jungle Book Resort

In the small village of Colem (Kulem), this resort offers activities ranging from jungle trekking to ziplining **(below)**. Visitors can stay overnight in the simple mud huts here.

NEED TO KNOW

Dudhsagar Falls: **MAP F4**; open 6:30am–5:00pm daily; adm (additional charge for photography)

Mahishasura Mardini Temple: **MAP E4**; Cormonem

Bhagwan Mahavir Wildlife Sanctuary: **MAP F4**; 0832 222 1505; open 7am–5pm daily; adm

Backwoods Camp: **MAP F3**; 0942 007 2007

Tambdi Surla Mahadev Temple, Sunset Point, Tambdi Surla Waterfall & Nature Interpretation Centre: **MAP F3**

Jungle Book Resort: **MAP F3**; 0982 212 1441

Devil's Canyon: **MAP F4**

■ Tickets to the wildlife sanctuary are available at the Nature Interpretation Centre.

■ Devil's Canyon may be closed at the end of the monsoons when the water levels are high.

7 Tambdi Surla Waterfall

Almost as high as Dudhsagar, this waterfall is 2 km (1.2 miles) northwest of Tambdi Surla. Adventure enthusiasts will enjoy trekking through the dense foliage and steep rocky trail, with the help of experienced guides to get to the base of this waterfall.

8 Nature Interpretation Centre

Located within the sanctuary, this centre provides information on the diverse array of plant and animal life to help visitors understand and learn more about the native flora and fauna that can be seen here.

10 Devil's Canyon

This scenic river gorge in the sanctuary consists of a zig-zagging mass of rock with underground passages. Visitors should be careful not to swim here as the undercurrents are quite strong and treacherous.

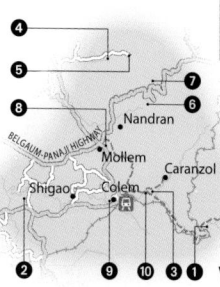

🔟⭐ **Margao and Around**

Goa's second most important city after Panaji, Margao (Madgaon) is the administrative and commercial capital of the South Goa district. Located nearby is Colva, one of the most developed beach resorts in South Goa. Inland from Margao, the villages of Loutolim and Chandor are home to several beautiful colonial *palacios*. Further east lies the small hamlet of Rachol, which originally was the site of an old fortress built by the Bijapur sultans.

① Church of the Holy Spirit

This towering Baroque church **(below)** has a grand interior with an impressive stucco ceiling, a gilded pulpit, Rococo altar and elegant altar-pieces in the transepts.

④ Braganza House

The impressive scale of Braganza House *(see pp36–7)*, and its magnificent interior, make it Goa's grandest mansion. Built by the Braganza family, the house was later divided into the east and west wings.

② Monte Hill

East of the church, a road winds up to Monte Hill. Although visitors cannot enter the chapel at the top of the hill, the views across Margao's rooftops of the southern coast from here are great.

⑤ Goa Chitra Museum

This ethnographic museum **(below)** is set on a working organic farm. It aims to promote the region's traditional agrarian lifestyle and has antique agricultural tools and artifacts on display.

⑥ Rachol Seminary

Spectacularly located on the summit of a hill, this seminary **(above)** has a fort-like façade, flanked by watchtowers. Adjacent to it is the Church of St Ignatius Loyola, dedicated to the eponymous saint. According to legend, bone fragments and a vial of his blood are enshrined near the entrance.

③ Figueiredo Mansion

Believed to be more than 500 years old, this mansion *(see p100)* has a narrow passage with disguised gun holes, below the building. The Figueiredo family used this as an escape tunnel when attacked by bandits.

Margao and Around

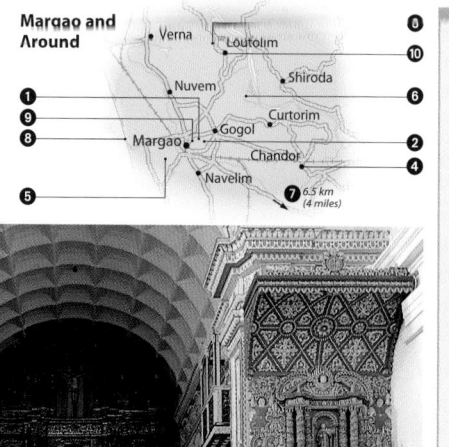

Verna · Loutolim
Nuvem · Shiroda
Curtorim
Margao · Gogol
Chandor
Navelim
6.5 km (4 miles)

10 Ancestral Goa
This model village (see p100) depicts Goan life from a bygone era. Here you'll find statues, miniature colonial homes and a laterite sculpture **(below)** of Mirabai.

7 Palácio do Deão

Built as a country house by Portuguese nobleman Jose Paulo de Almeida, this colonial mansion (see p100) with its tropical gardens was once a retreat for the colony's viceroys. Visitors can enjoy lunch on the terrace, overlooking the Kushavati River.

8 Utorda Beach

One of Goa's most serene and cleanest beaches, Utorda's proximity to Margao makes it an ideal summer retreat. It is dotted with seafood cafés.

9 Sat Burnzam Ghor

Named after the original seven gables on its roof, this mansion is Goa's only surviving example of a house with a pyramidal roof.

NEED TO KNOW

Church of the Holy Spirit:
MAP B5; Holy Spirit Rd, Borda; 0832 271 4005; open 9am–noon, 4–7pm daily

Figueiredo Mansion:
MAP B4; Loutolim; 0832 277 7028; open 9am–5pm daily; adm; www.figueiredo house.com

Braganza House: **MAP C6**; Chandor; 0832 278 4201; open 9am–6pm daily; adm

Goa Chitra Museum: **MAP B5**; Benaulim; 0832 657 0877; open 9am–6pm daily; adm; www.goachitra.com

Rachol Seminary: **MAP C5**; 0832 277 6052; www.racholseminarygoa.org

Palácio do Deão: **MAP E4**; Quepem; 0832 266 4029; open 10am–5pm Sat–Thu; www.palaciododeao.com

Utorda Beach: **MAP D4**

Sat Burnzam Ghor:
MAP B5; 0832 266 4029

Ancestral Goa: **MAP B4**; Loutolim; 0832 227 7034; open 9am–6pm daily; adm; www.ancestralgoa.com

Braganza House

1 East and West Wing
The mansion is divided into two separate wings, occupied by different branches of the Braganza family. The descendants of Antonio Elzario Sant'Anna Pereira occupy the east wing, while the Menezes Braganzas live in the west wing.

2 Hallway
A long and elegantly furnished hallway lies just behind the double-storey Portuguese-style façade of the house. It is lined with 28 bay windows and overlooks a well-maintained garden.

Baroque rosewood four-poster bed

3 Dining Hall
In the east wing, a rosewood dining table, meant to be an exact replica of the one at Buckingham Palace, fills the first floor dining hall of this sprawling mansion.

4 Chapel
The Braganza Pereira's private Baroque-style chapel in the east wing has a number of treasures including a gold-and-diamond-encrusted fingernail of St Francis Xavier (see p27) on its main altar.

5 Guest Bedroom
This room is dominated by a large rosewood four-poster bed. At its foot is a rosewood two-seater.

6 Stairway
A monumental double staircase forms the core of the house. The staircase connects the lower entrance level to the furnished top floors of the east wing, which comprise a series of interconnecting salons, dining halls, reception rooms, and the family's private chambers, ranged around a central courtyard.

7 Great Salon
The grandest room in the mansion is the Great Salon or ballroom. The walls as well as the floors are of Italian marble, and match the upholstry, while Belgian crystal chandeliers hang from the floral-patterned zinc ceiling. The highlight here is a pair of matching high-backed chairs, bearing the Braganza coat of arms, which was presented to the Braganza Pereira household by King Dom Luís of Portugal.

The splendid Great Salon

GOA'S PORTUGUESE ARCHITECTURE

Charming Sunaparanta, Goa Centre for the Arts

Goa's countryside is dotted with grand colonial mansions, built by wealthy land-owning Goan gentry. The homes of these local aristocrats were built in the traditional style of the region, with central courtyards, pyramidal *balcões* (porches) and unique oyster-shell window shutters. The furniture and interior decor, however, were largely European. Today, the beautiful Belgian chandeliers, Venetian cut-glass, gilded mirrors, antique Baroque-style rosewood furniture and Chinese porcelain, all displayed inside, provide a fascinating picture of the tastes and lifestyles of a vanished era.

TOP 10 INDO-PORTUGUESE HOUSES IN GOA

1 Figueiredo Mansion (see p34), Loutolim

2 Salvador da Costa House, Loutolim

3 Deshprabhu House, Pernem

4 Casa dos Mirandos, Loutolim

5 Sat Burnzam Ghor (see p35), Margao

6 Loyola Furtado Mansion, Chinchinim

7 Braganza House (see p34), Chandor

8 Palácio do Deão (see p35), Quepem

9 Sunaparanta, Goa Centre for the Arts (see p23), Altinho

10 Solar dos Colacos Ribandar

8 Menezes Braganza Salon

The west wing opens into a salon. A collection of exquisite Chinese porcelain is displayed here, where a large vase takes pride of place.

9 Library

With over 5,000 leather-bound books, mostly collected by renowned journalist and freedom fighter Luis de Menezes Braganza (1878–1938), the west wing library is considered one of Goa's finest and biggest private collections. There's also a set of four finely upholstered chairs called tête-à-têtes or love seats carrying their flamboyant owner's initials FXB (Francis Xavier Braganza).

10 Family Portraits

A number of 17th- and 18th-century portraits of family

Portraits of family members

members can be seen around the house. A portrait of the grandfather of Luis de Menezes Braganza, Francis Xavier de Menezes Braganza, one of the few aristocrats to oppose Portuguese rule, hangs in the west wing ballroom.

TOP 10 ⭐ Palolem, Agonda and Around

Famous for its spectacular sunsets, Palolem is the ideal destination for a quiet holiday, away from central Goa's crowded beaches. North of Palolem is Agonda, which is even quieter than its neighbour, while Galgibaga has a beautiful stretch of virgin sand, shaded by casuarina trees. Also worth exploring is Rivona's Buddhist heritage and Usgalimal's prehistoric rock art. West of Palolem is Cotigao's wildlife sanctuary, known for its tranquil beauty.

1 Agonda Beach

This white sandy beach (see p99), set between two cliffs, is a sought-after destination. It is famous as the nesting site for Olive Ridley turtles.

2 Palolem Island Reserve

Just off Palolem Beach, this island reserve has retained its biodiversity. Home to birds of prey, the island offers breath-taking ocean views. Dolphins or turtles can be spotted from a boat.

3 Cola Beach

To the north of Agonda is one of Goa's most secluded beaches, Cola (see p46). Visitors can opt to stay in Rajasthani-style tent camps on the beach. There's also a freshwater lagoon here.

5 Netravali

This village is famous for its unique Bubble Lake. The Mainapi waterfall **(above)**, lies within a nearby wildlife sanctuary, which abounds in rich flora and fauna.

4 Butterfly Beach

A short boat ride away from the Palolem coast this beach **(below)** takes its name from the exotic butterflies that can be spotted here (see p100). It is known for its rich aquatic life and sunset views.

GOA'S WESTERN GHATS

The landscape around Cabo de Rama is the only place in the state where the forest-cloaked Western Ghats detour to meet the sea. Goa's most important topographical feature, the ghats make up almost 20 per cent of the state's landmass. This area has an abundance of flora and fauna and is known for its rich tropical biodiversity.

6 Galgibaga

A remote white sandy bay, Galgibaga or Turtle Beach (see p47) is one of best known nesting sites for Olive Ridley turtles. The northern end of the beach forms the turtles' habitat.

7 Rivona Buddhist Caves

These rock-cut caves, also known as Pandava Caves, were created in the 7th-century CE by Buddhist monks. The highlight here is the carved laterite *pitha*, the seat of the teacher.

10 Cabo de Rama

South of the fishing village of Betul is the Cabo de Rama (Cape Rama) promontory **(above)**. It is named after Rama, hero of the *Ramayana*, who is believed to have stayed here during his exile.

NEED TO KNOW

Agonda Beach & Cola Beach: **MAP D5**

Palolem Island Reserve & Butterfly Beach: **MAP D6**

Netravali: **MAP E5**

Galgibaga: **MAP D6**

Rivona Buddhist Caves: **MAP E5**

Cabo de Rama: **MAP D5**; Canacona; open 9am–5:30pm daily

Usgalimal Rock Carvings: **MAP E5**

Cotigao Wildlife Sanctuary: **MAP E6**; Canacona; 0832 296 5601; open 7am–5:30pm daily; adm

■ **Cabo de Rama** features the ruins of a Hindu fortress that fell to the Portuguese in 1763. The ramparts on the western side offer great views.

Palolem, Agonda and Around

Cuncolim · Rivona · Curdi
Betul
Cabo de Rama · Naquerim · Jagvi
Palolem
Canacona Chaudi

8 Usgalimal Rock Carvings

Many well-preserved petroglyphs, carved on laterite rock were found here in 1993. Believed to date back to the Stone Age, the carvings include birds and hunting scenes.

9 Cotigao Wildlife Sanctuary

Perfect for tree lovers, this vast reserve (see p100) of mixed deciduous woodland has plenty of birdlife **(left)**, but you are less likely to spot other wildlife here.

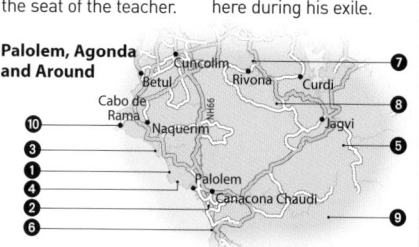

The Top 10 of Everything

Splendid *reredos* with panels depicting scenes from the life of St Catherine at Sé Cathedral

ᴛᴏᴘ**10** Moments in History

A scene from *Os Lusiadas*, depicting Vasco da Gama's arrival in Goa

(1) Mythological Goa

There are many legends about the creation of "Gomanta", "Govapuri", or present-day Goa. Despite the lack of historical evidence, Hindu mythology claims that Parashurama, an incarnation of god Vishnu, carved out this region after pushing out the sea with his arrows.

(2) Circa 300 BC: The Mauryas

Around this time, Goa was part of the Mauryan Empire under emperor Ashoka. He tried to convert the local people to Buddhism but after his death in 232 BC, much of these efforts fell flat as Goa was subesequently ruled by various Hindu dynasties for the next seven centuries. The Kadambas rose to power in AD 420, ushering in the first phase of the Golden Age of Goa.

(3) 1352: The Sultanate

Years of tolerance and prosperity came to an end in 1352 as the Muslim Bahmanis took

A proselytizing priest during the Inquisition

over. This was followed by a period of religious and cultural persecution and all symbols of the Hindu Kadamba legacy were destroyed, except the temple in Tambdi Surla *(see p33)*.

(4) 1498: Arrival of Vasco da Gama

Captained by Vasco da Gama, the Portuguese became the first Europeans to control trade routes to India. In 1543, after years of resistance, the sultan ceded large areas of Goa to them.

(5) 1560: Golden Goa to Goan Inquisition

By the end of the 16th century, Goa prospered under Portuguese rule. However, the initial focus on trade was replaced by the arrival of the *Santo Officio* (Holy Office), better known as the Inquisition. One of the most brutal examples of cultural bigotry, it was conceived to target the "new Christians". Over the next 200 years, the Inquisition executed thousands of "heretics" of all faiths.

The Marathas
6 In 1664, the Portuguese temporarily lost a major part of their Goan territory to the Marathas, while the British continued to contest for the same. In 1739, in exchange for the Marathas withdrawal from Goa, the Portuguese were forced to sign a treaty and ceded large areas of their colony near Bombay.

1787: Pinto Revolt
7 Inspired by the propaganda used in the French Revolution, three priests from the Pinto clan conspired to overthrow the Portuguese. The plot was discovered, and the conspirators were tortured and executed, or sent away to Portugal.

1843: Old Goa to New Goa
8 New Goa (present-day Panaji) became the new official capital, leaving Old Goa deserted.

The first Republic Day after Liberation

Attempts at Liberation
9 Goa remained under Portuguese control even after India became independent in 1947. The Nehru government maintained that Goa, along with other Portuguese-occupied territories should be handed over to India. In 1961, after several requisitions to the Salazar regime failed, Indian troops marched in and were able to "liberate" Goa.

Present-day Goa
10 Since it was declared the 25th state of India in 1987, the tourism industry has flourished, making Goa a sought-after destination. The airport at Mopa, which opened in late 2022, is expected to boost the state's economy and meet the rising demand of tourism.

TOP 10 FAMOUS PERSONALITIES

Famous artist, Subodh Kerkar

1 Kesarbai Kerkar (1892–1977)
Awarded the Sangeet Natak Akademi award, she went on to become one of the most celebrated *khayal* (a kind of Indian classical vocal music) singers.

2 Deenanath Mangeshkar (1900–42)
This Hindustani classical vocalist was also a famous Marathi theatre actor.

3 Mario Miranda (1926–2011)
This famous cartoonist shot to fame after his work got published in *The Illustrated Weekly of India*.

4 Dilip Sardesai (1940–2007)
A former test cricketer, he is regarded as India's best batsman against spin.

5 Pundalik Naik (1952–)
The Sahitya Akademi award winner shot to fame with his novel *Acchev* (*The Upheaval*, 1977), the first Konkani novel to be translated into English.

6 Remo Fernandes (1953–)
A popular singer-composer, he was a big part of the Indi-pop music revolution of the 1990s.

7 Subodh Kerkar (1959–)
Aiming to make art more accessible for the masses, this eminent artist founded the Museum of Goa *(see p90)*.

8 Wendell Rodricks (1960–2020)
A fashion designer, environmental activist and a writer, he has restored his 450-year-old house and converted it to the Moda Goa Museum *(see p91)*.

9 Jayanti Naik (1962–)
Winner of the Sahitya Akademi award, this writer and translator is committed to the preservation of Konkani folklore.

10 Bruno Coutinho (1969–)
A former Indian football captain, he has received the Arjuna Award for outstanding achievement in the field.

🔟 Places of Worship

in 1619. The central pediment and belfry were built later to accommodate the huge bell brought from Old Goa. The chapel in the south transept is dedicated to St Francis Xavier.

3 Church of St Cajetan

In the 17th century, Pope Urban III sent Italian priests from the Theatine Order to Golconda. They were refused entry there so they settled in Old Goa. In 1651, they erected a church (see p25) dedicated to their founder, St Cajetan, modelled on St Peter's in Rome. The dome and Baroque interior are in the form of a Greek cross.

4 Church and Monastery of St Augustine

Once the largest church (see p24) in India, with a five-storeyed façade, St Augustine's now lies in ruins. The church was abandoned in 1835, and excavations in 1989 revealed eight chapels and four altars. It is believed that in the 17th century there were also grand staircases, and a library that rivalled the one in Oxford. Today, all that remains is its bell tower.

5 Maruti Temple

MAP L3 ▪ Nanu Tarkar Pednekar Rd, Altinho, Panaji ▪ Open 6am–8pm

A striking edifice atop Altinho Hill, this temple looks beautiful at night when it is lit up. The presiding deity here is the monkey-god Hanuman who can be seen through a tiny hole in the basement wall.

Gilded high altar at Sé Cathedral

1 Sé Cathedral

The magnificent Sé Cathedral (see p25) has a Tuscan-style façade, flanked by a bell tower. The tower houses the Golden Bell, which rang out during the Inquisition's dreaded *auto da fé* trials, held in the front square. The *pièce de résistance* of the Corinthian interior is the altar, dedicated to St Catherine of Alexandria.

2 Church of Our Lady of the Immaculate Conception

This church (see p20) is Panaji's most distinctive landmark. The whitewashed Baroque façade of the present church and its twin towers were constructed

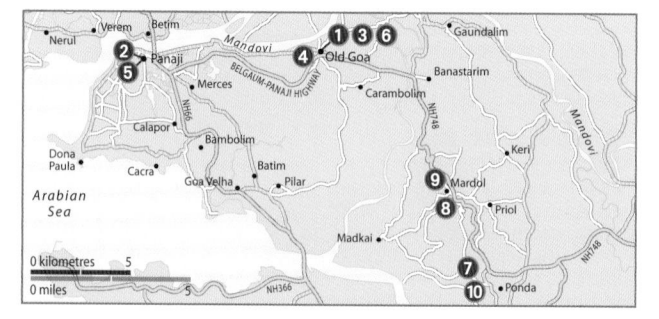

Baroque interior with floral frescoes at the Church of St Francis of Assisi

6 Church of St Francis of Assisi

A rare example of the Portuguese Manueline style, this church *(see p24)* has a beautifully carved doorway. A pair of navigator's globes and a Greek cross (the emblem of all Portuguese ships) embellish the door. The painted panels in the chancel depict scenes from the saint's life. The church is no longer used for worship.

7 Naguesh Temple

Dedicated to Lord Shiva, this temple *(see p30)* has an ancient water tank, built in a way that the reflection of the idol of Nagesh can be seen when standing at certain angles around the tank. The temple does not allow entry to foreigners.

8 Lakshmi Narasimha Temple

MAP D3 ■ Pharmacy College Rd, National Highway 4A, Ponda ■ Open 6:30am–12:45pm & 4:30–8:30pm daily

Surrounded by a forest, this is one of Goa's most attractive temples, with a sacred tank and an elaborate gateway. The majestic idol of Narasimha, Vishnu's man-lion incarnation, was brought here in the 1560s from South Goa's Salcete *taluka* (sub-district).

9 Shri Mangueshi Temple

A vividly painted elephant on wheels stands at the entrance to this 18th-century temple *(see p84)*, dedicated to Shiva. Inside, Belgian chandeliers hang from the ceiling, while the courtyard has a sacred *tulsi* (basil) plant growing in a green urn. There's also a seven-storeyed lamp tower here.

10 Shantadurga Temple

Goa's most popular shrine *(see p81)* was built by Shahuji, the grandson of Maratha chief Shivaji. This russet- and cream-coloured temple has an unusual pagoda-style roof, dominated by a five-storeyed octagonal lamp tower, unique to Goa. Embossed silver screens shield the main sanctuary, which houses the deity of Shantadurga (a form of Shiva's consort Parvati).

Shantadurga Temple

🔟 Beaches

1 Vagator
Beautiful Vagator's crescent-shaped bay is known for its small coves. The main beach *(see p14)* is split into Big and Little Vagator by a seaside headland. To the south is Ozran or Little Vagator, accessible by a steep path, which attracts party-goers in the evening. Its defining feature is the rock carving of Lord Shiva's face.

2 Cola
Also known as "Khola" beach, this is perhaps one of Goa's most beautiful beaches

Aerial view of charming Cola Beach

(see p38) with coconut groves and Rajasthani-style tents. The freshwater lagoon here, makes a great swimming spot. Consult a lifeguard for the best places to swim at the beach.

3 Ashvem
Goa's current hot spot, Ashvem *(see p18)* has become the place to soak up the sun, sand and surf. Its serene waters, eclectic beach shack restaurants, chic beachfront clubs and boutiques have made it the choice of celebrities. It is also known as one of the best spots to swim, dine and dance.

4 Majorda
MAP A5 ■ **Greenland Horse Racing: 9822586502**
North of Colva, Majorda has a wide beach dotted with luxury hotels. Relatively peaceful and mostly crowd-free, this beach can be reached by crossing makeshift wooden bridges. It is the only place in Goa where visitors can ride a horse on the beach.

5 Arambol
Lively Arambol *(see p18)* has a freshwater lagoon that is fed by hot springs and is perfect for swimming. It is popular with those seeking active outdoor recreation and holistic therapies such as yoga and reiki, and is also known for its vibrant nightlife.

6 Mobor
MAP D5 ■ **Betty's Place Boat Trips: www.bettysgoa.com**
With its backdrop of jungle-covered hills, Mobor's golden white sands feature a number of luxury resorts including the famous Leela Goa *(see p114)*. There are little stalls selling souvenirs and trinkets. Visitors can go on river cruises as well as amazing dolphin-spotting and birdwatching trips.

A wooden bridge leading to the oceanfront shacks at Mandrem

7 Mandrem

A quiet fishing village with a beautiful location and a pristine beach *(see p18)*, Mandrem's relaxed ambience is ideal for solitude-seekers. Small wooden bridges help visitors to cross a narrow creek that runs parallel to the coastline, and connects to the beach shacks, which line the shore.

8 Galgibaga

Fringed by towering casuarina trees, tranquil Galgibaga *(see p39)* is a favoured breeding ground for the critically endangered Olive Ridley turtles. In November, the turtles lay their eggs, often on the same spot where they themselves had hatched. The hatchling numbers though have decreased over the years.

9 Agonda

Picturesque Agonda Beach *(see p99)* is great for lazing under the sun and treating yourself to some amazing food and cocktails. Visitors can choose to enjoy a swim or engage in watersports, particularly canoeing, which is quite popular here. The turtle centre here helps conserve the Olive Ridley turtle eggs.

10 Querim

Tucked away at the northernmost tip of Goa far from the buzz of other beaches, gorgeous Querim (or Keri) is the ultimate hideaway. With its empty stretches of soft sand and clear waters *(see p19)* it is the ideal place for sunbathing and swimming. It also has a sea cave that can be explored on foot. Wear sturdy shoes as the rocks can be quite slippery inside the cave.

Lovely, unspoiled beach at Querim

🔟 Unique Experiences

Mud bathing at Chorão Island

1 Get a Mud Bath
Soul Travelling: www.soultravelling.in
The perfect way to relax sore muscles, exfoliate the skin and draw out impurities, mud baths are a popular activity in Goa. Soul Travelling provides tours of Chorão Island *(see p71)*, where, after exploring the local sites, you get to immerse yourself in a lake of healing mud.

2 Go Mangrove Kayaking
Explore North Goa's beautiful and biodiverse mangrove forests by taking a guided kayaking tour. While paddling your way through the meandering waterways, you will get an insight into the rich

Exploring Goa's mangroves in a kayak

ecosystem thriving within its dense mangrove forests. Konkan Explorers *(see p20)* offer a thrilling mangrove kayaking experience.

3 Try Cashew Feni
Cazulo Premium Feni: https://cazulofeni.com
Easily the most popular alcoholic beverage in Goa, cashew *feni* or *kaju feni (see p59)*, as it is locally known, has been a staple for Goans for more than 400 years. This spirit is made from distilling the juice from ripened cashew apples. Cazulo Premium Feni has an experience centre that helps visitors to discover the world of *feni*. It involves a walk through a cashew orchard, a visit to a traditional distillery, a tasting session and finally, an alfresco meal under the stars.

4 Join a Psytrance Party
Known as the home of trance music in Goa, HillTop *(see p94)* is a must-do for a night of music and partying. Surrounded by towering palm trees and decorated with neon lights and psychedelic art, this iconic venue in Vagator has an idyllic setting. The whole neon party vibe is not the only reason it's a hit with trance lovers. It features some of the best musical talent with the most sought-after international artists performing here, sometimes non-stop for 24 hours.

A Malabar trogon sighting in Goa

5 Enjoy Birdwatching
Mrugaya Xpeditions: www. mrugayaxpeditions.com

Goa is a birder's paradise with many species endemic to peninsular India as well as many wintering species from farther north calling it home. Operators such as Mrugaya Xpeditions offer nature trails and birding tours throughout Goa.

6 Stay in an Indo-Portuguese Mansion

Step back in time by staying overnight in an Indo-Portuguese mansion. These houses are a testament to Goa's rich cultural heritage, blending Indian and Portuguese influences in its architecture, design and ambience. Many Indo-Portuguese houses in Fontainhas and Mapusa have been converted into boutique guesthouses or homestays. The hosts, often locals, are passionate about showcasing their heritage. The 16th-century Figueiredo Mansion (see p115), earlier a museum, has now opened its doors to guests.

7 Take a Cooking Class
Alila Diwa Goa: www.alila hotels.com

Known for its delectable blend of spices, fresh seafood and unique cooking techniques, Goan cuisine offers a wide array of dishes that reflect the state's diverse cultural influences. Join a cooking class to learn more about the region's vibrant food culture. At the Alila Diwa Goa (see p114) guests can select their choice of the morning's fresh catch and then learn to cook a Goan delicacy at the Alila Cooking School.

8 Dine in a Forest
Wildernest Goa: www. wildernest-goa.com

As the culinary scene continues to flourish in Goa, an increasing number of restaurants now offer elevated private dining experiences. Wildernest Goa (see p121) in Chorla Ghat (see p70) is one of the best. Here, guests are treated to colourful dance performances followed by a grand jungle buffet featuring local dishes made with fresh ingredients.

9 See an Interactive Film
Make It Happen: www. makeithappen.co.in/tour/guardian-spirits-of-goa

A beautiful interactive film, *Guardian Spirits of Goa* chronicles the age-old practice of paying obeisance to the protector spirits that are believed to exist in every corner of Goa. Make It Happen organizes regular screenings of the film.

10 Watch a Football Match
MAP D4 ■ Pandit Jawaharlal Nehru Stadium, Margao

The Fatorda Stadium, officially known as the Pandit Jawaharlal Nehru Stadium, is the home ground of the FC Goa football club. This state-of-the-art facility has hosted India's qualifiers for the FIFA World Cup and the AFC Asian Cup. Head to the stadium to watch a match live.

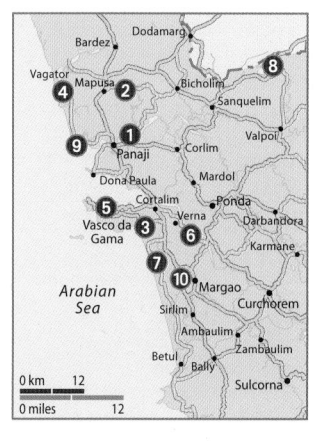

 Outdoor Activities

① Surfing
Surf School, Vaayu Kula:
www.vaayukula.com

Goa's beaches are mostly popular for surfing, although the sea here is also ideal for other watersports. There are a number of surfing schools, such as Vaayu Kula *(see p18)*, Octopus Surf School and Surf Wala in Arambol, which offer instruction for both beginners and experienced surfers.

Paragliding over Arambol Beach

② Paragliding
Rainbow Paragliding:
www.rainbowparagliding.com

Thrill-seekers can book a tandem glide and soar along the shores of Arambol and Querim, enjoying some of the best views of Goa as they go. You can learn how to fly in strong wind conditions, land and ridge soar. More experienced flyers can take independent, advanced flying courses as well.

③ Rafting
Goa Rafting: 8805 727 230;
www.goarafting.com

White-water rafting on the Mhadei River is a popular activity from June to September. Goa Rafting organizes trips in season at 9:30am and 2:30pm on Grade 2 and 3 (fairly easy) rapids.

④ Kayaking
**Make It Happen: www.
makeithappen.co.in**

Palolem and Cola beaches are considered best for kayaking. Make It Happen offer great mangrove river kayaking tours.

⑤ Nature Walks
**Khoj-aao! Adventures: www.
khojaao.com**

Goa offers plenty of nature excursions, birdwatching tours and camping expeditions under the stars from October to April. Some of the top birdwatching spots include Cotigao Wildlife Sanctuary *(see p39)*, Salim Ali Bird Sanctuary *(see p84)* and Bhagwan Mahavir Wildlife Sanctuary *(see p32)*.

⑥ Kitesurfing
Kitesurfing Goa: Montego Bay Resort, Morjim Beach; 0750 713 0099
www.kitesurfinggoa.com

Kitesurfing is a dynamic form of wave-riding. Boards are short and the rider holds handles attached to cables and a kite. From January to April, Morjim Beach *(see p18)* is a major hub for this sport.

⑦ Stand Up Paddle Boarding (SUP)
**Atlantis Watersports: www.atlantis
watersports.com**

This sport has gained a lot of popularity over the years, with boards tuition and guided paddles offered by schools. The ideal months for SUP is from October to May.

Hikers on a scenic trail in Netravali

Bungee jumping at Mayem Lake

8 Bungee Jumping
Jumpin Heights: Mayem Lake, Bicholim; www.jumpin heights.com

For an adrenaline rush like no other take a 55 m (180 ft) leap from Goa's only bungee jumping platform, which overlooks the stunning Mayem Lake in North Goa. A complimentary video of your dive is included.

9 ATV Rides
ATV Adventures Goa: 0982 306 8599

All-terrain vehicles are an exciting way to explore muddy trails and off-the-beaten path sights. There are several tracks in North Goa. Wear sports shoes or closed-toe shoes.

10 Hiking
Goa Jungle Adventure: www.goajungle.com

Several thrilling hiking options are available for adventurers to explore Goa's captivating landscapes. Some of the best trails are at Chorla Ghat (see p84), Netravali (see p38) and Dudhsagar Falls (see p32). Hiking is not advisable during the monsoon.

TOP 10 SPECIAL INTEREST ACTIVITIES

Go-Karting on a track in Goa

1 Go-Karting
The tracks in Nuvem village and Arpora are the best. Check www.gokarting goa.com for more information.

2 Soccer
Some of the Indian Super League matches (from November to March), are played at Fatorda Stadium. Goa's main professional football team is FC Goa.

3 Scuba Diving
Goa Diving (www.goadiving.com), a PADI dive centre, has guided dives to shipwreck sites.

4 Fishing
There are a number of boats that will take visitors out fishing for the day. Check www.johnboattours.com for fishing trips.

5 Parasailing
Baga and Calangute beaches are great for parasailing. October to May is the best time for this popular watersport.

6 Dance and Aerial Yoga
Omaggio Goa (see p15) in Anjuna has yoga and dance classes for all ages.

7 Boat Trips
Cruises of every sort are popular on the Mandovi. Konkan Explorers (www.konkanexplorers.com) offer several eco-conscious marine excursions.

8 Dolphin Spotting
Palolem, Morjim or Sinquerim are the best beaches to catch a glimpse of the Indo-Pacific humpback dolphin.

9 Bicycle Tours
Avid cyclists can opt for an interesting bicycle tour to explore Old Goa, Chorão and Divar Islands.

10 Climbing Rock Walls
A great indoor location for rock climbing is the Equilibrium Climbing Station (www.equilibriumclimbing.com) in Anjuna. It has a huge practice wall.

Following pages Spectacular view of the Dudhsagar Falls

⭐10 **Children's Attractions**

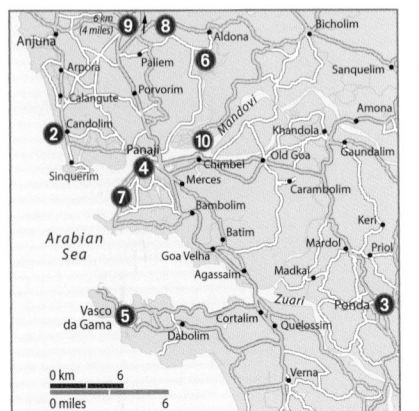

① Dolphin Spotting
Terra Conscious: www.terraconscious.com ▪ John Boat Tours: www.johnboattours.com
Some of the best beaches for dolphin spotting are Palolem, Sinquerim, Baga and Morjim. A number of eco-conscious operators such as Terra Conscious and John's Boat Tours organize educational dolphin safaris.

② Splashdown Water Park
MAP H4 ▪ Calangute–Anjuna Main Rd, Anjuna ▪ Open 10:30am–6pm ▪ Adm ▪ www.splashdowngoa.com
This water park boasts a number of high-velocity rides (multi-passenger as well as solo) down slides and chutes or tubes. Rides such as the "Curly Wurly" water slide and the "Tad Pool" have been designed for small children.

③ Spice Plantations
Central Goa's spice plantations (see p30) offer a delightful opportunity for a family day-out. Most of the spice farms in and around Ponda have guided tours in English, which is a wonderful way to learn about organically grown spices, herbs, fruits and crops. This is usually followed by a traditional Goan lunch buffet. July to March are the best months to visit the plantations.

④ Skateboarding
MAP J4 ▪ Miramar Skatepark at Youth Hostel, Panaji ▪ 8329 911510
This 298 sq m (3,200 sq ft) skatepark is a dedicated space for eight to ten simultaneous skaters, with a remarkable variety of ramps to practice on. It provides great entertainment for the kids and has amazing ocean views. There are also skate camps for both beginners and advanced skaters at very affordable rates.

A skater at Miramar Skatepark

5 Naval Aviation Museum

Goa's Naval Aviation Museum *(see p100)* boasts 15 types of aircrafts and exhibits such as scaled models of aircraft carriers, *INS Viraat* and *INS Vikrant*. The two-storeyed indoor gallery features rare photographs and information about key battles in which the Indian Naval and Air force participated. The evolution of the uniforms worn by Navy personnel are also well documented. The outdoor exhibits include several decommissioned aircrafts, which are on display in the museum's huge park.

Statues of craftsmen at work, Ancestral Goa

6 Kayaking

Olaulim Backyards: www. olaulimgoa.com ■ Make it Happen: www.makeithappen.in

One of the most popular activities, kayaking is a great way for families to have a fabulous experience on the water and it doesn't take much time to learn at all. It's also a wonderful way to explore the rivers and backwaters of Goa and witness the local life and culture of India's sunshine state. Kids will enjoy getting up close and personal with the local flora and fauna.

7 Goa Science Centre & Planetarium

MAP J6 ■ Marine Highway, Miramar, Panaji ■ Open 10am–6pm daily ■ Adm ■ www.goasciencecentre. org.in

The fantastic Goa Science Centre & Planetarium is the perfect place to experience a fun day. The science centre has two interactive galleries to explain the basic concepts of physics to kids. In addition, there is a 3D theatre and a dome-shaped planetarium. The outdoor park also has life-size models of dinosaurs.

8 Ancestral Goa

This unique model village *(see p35)* showcases Goan life and culture as it was a hundred years ago through miniature Portuguese colonial homes and life-size statues of tradesmen and craftsmen. Other attractions include the footprint of Big Foot on a rock and the longest laterite sculpture of Mirabai, a poet and devotee of Lord Krishna.

9 Young Explorers Club

Khoj-aao! Adventures: www. khojaao.com

Children will enjoy exploring different ecosystems over a six-week learning session. They can participate in interactive nature-related activities and games to learn and discover more about Goa's flora and fauna.

10 Salim Ali Bird Sanctuary

This sanctuary *(see p84)* was named after Dr Salim Moizzudin Abdul Ali, one of the country's foremost ornithologists. In addition to colourful kingfishers and egrets, you may also spot the bulbous-headed mudskipper leaping above the water. The mangrove swamps can be explored by taking a boat ride in a dug-out canoe. It is best to visit early in the morning or just before sunset.

🔟 Nightlife

Dancefloor packed with revellers at the Sinq Night Club

1 HillTop

Set in a neon coconut grove, HillTop *(see p94)* transforms into a prime destination for Goa's trance party scene on some evenings. Apart from its wild New Year and Christmas rave parties, which span over three or four days, it is famous for its weekly Sunday sessions when international DJs spin psychedelic-trance beats until 10pm and on Fridays when the focus shifts to techno and house.

2 House of Chapora

Fans of electronic music will not want to miss visiting this trendy club *(see p94)*, which is located close to the Chapora jetty in Vagator. The resident and visiting DJs here keep the crowds on their feet by spinning their sets late into the night.

3 Club Tito's

Baga's legendary nightlife is mainly attributed to the iconic Tito's *(see p94)*. Every Saturday night, revellers descend on the dance floor to enjoy pulsating retro and Bollywood hits. Guest DJs feature throughout the season. Next door is Mambo's, which gets packed with a lively crowd most nights. Hip-hop, and techno dominate after 11pm here.

4 Sinq Night Club

Created as a one stop destination for partygoers, Sinq *(see p94)* features four entertainment zones – a chic nightclub, a bistro with an Irish pub ambience, a poolside deck and private cabanas – that create the ultimate party venue. There's an open-air poolside lounge with a discotheque as well. Resident DJs spin mainstream dance tracks several nights a week.

5 Rockwaves Goa

MAP H3 ▪ Gawde Wado, Morjim ▪ 8888787632 ▪ Open 24 hours daily

Situated right by the beach in Morjim, Rockwaves Goa is a friendly beachside bar that particularly comes alive at night with lively parties and other trendy events. On Saturday nights there's a popular Vortex Crew party in season.

Striking exterior of LPK Waterfront

6 Shiva Valley

Known as the temple of trance, this large shack *(see p94)* attracts a huge crowd. Every Tuesday it remains packed mostly due to its psychedelic trance parties, which kick off from 5pm and continue well beyond midnight. Besides Tuesdays, Full Moon Night parties are also a big hit here. It has hosted big-name DJs, such as Earthling, Avalon, Tristan, Nigel, Ajja, Raja Ram.

7 Ecstatic Dance Shunya

Since 2021, ShunyaWellness in Arambol has been organizing dance parties that have become very popular in recent times. This international Ecstatic dance (or free form dance) venue *(see p94)* and community hosts dance events twice a week with resident and experienced guest DJs from all over the world. Smoking and drinking is not allowed but there is a lovely vegetarian café and a tea ceremony corner.

8 LPK Waterfront

MAP J6 ▪ Nerul Rd, Opposite Bank of India, Nerul ▪ 0932 673 3295 ▪ Open 9:30pm–3:30am daily

Set against the backdrop of a 400-year-old church on the banks of the Nerul, LPK or Love Passion Karma is a fashionable Goan nightspot. Constructed mainly out of mud and stone, sculpted terracotta statues can be seen all around. Groove to the latest Bollywood hits here. The deck provides a great chill-out area.

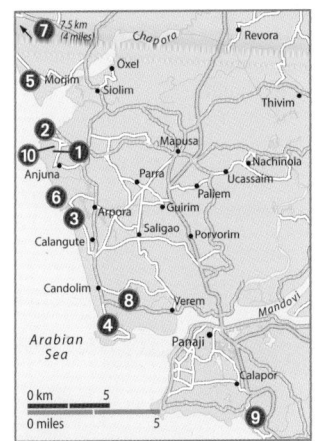

9 Leopard Valley

One of the biggest open-air venues in India, Leopard Valley *(see p102)* is a high-octane nightclub featuring a 7-m (22-ft) high DJ stage. Groove to the best of EDM and Goa trance amid 3D laser light shows, pyrotechnics and firepits. The main parties are held here on Friday nights. Guest DJs include Eve Carey of Ministry of Sound fame, MV Cliff and Dan Booth.

10 Hideaway Café and Bar

The lovely Hideaway Café and Bar *(see p94)* in Vagator is an inviting place with a friendly atmosphere and lots of energy. It hosts weekly gigs by artists from across the country. This restaurant-meets-B&B offers hearty food and great cocktails. The menu features a variety of cuisines from around the world, including Italian, Mexican and Asian.

🔟 Goan Cuisine

1 Xacuti
A staple found on the menu of most Goan restaurants is *xacuti*. The complex flavour that defines this chicken curry comes from the use of an elaborate number of spices and ingredients including poppy seeds, dessicated coconut and red chillies.

Fish prepared in *recheado* masala

2 Recheado
Essentially a spice paste, the *recheado* is used to season seafood, usually mackerel, often prawns and pomfret. The whole fish is slit down the middle and cleaned, stuffed with flavoursome *recheado* and then fried in hot oil to be served as an appetizer. Some vegetables are also cooked using the same masala.

3 Cafreal
The chicken is usually marinated overnight with spices, such as ginger, garlic, onion, mace, cinnamon, green chillies and fresh coriander, the latter brings about its signature green colour. Fried or grilled the following day, this dish is accompanied by potatoes, lemon wedges and salad.

4 Sorpotel
An essential in any Goan celebration, the preparation for this stew begins days in advance as it is believed that the flavour of the curry gets better as it ages. Recipes differ from one kitchen to the other, but the traditional version is made from boneless pork and pork offal – liver, tongue, heart – though modern variations use other meat as well.

5 Bebinca
There are various stories regarding the origin of this dessert but Goans love their *bebinca* and it is widely accepted as the "queen" of Goan desserts. This traditional cake is prepared in layers (the numbers range from seven to 16) using simple ingredients such as plain flour, coconut milk, sugar, egg yolk and *ghee* (clarified butter).

6 Vindaloo
This curry came to India with the Portuguese and the name itself is a distortion of their popular dish *carne de vinha d'alhos*. The use of dry roasted spices such as mustard, fennel and coriander seeds plus red chillies (courtesy the Portuguese) and peppercorns gives the *vindaloo* its characteristic heat. The spice is balanced by the use of vinegar, tamarind paste and jaggery.

Portuguese-influenced pork *vindaloo* curry

Fiery prawn *balchao*

7 Balchao

The origins of *balchao* lie in Macau, which was once a Portuguese colony. A blend of chillies, ground spices and tomatoes is pickled with either coconut or *feni* vinegar, which lends the mixture its signature acidic taste. The paste is then used to make a curry with pork, fish or prawns.

8 Sanna

This steamed, spongy rice cake is a Goan staple that has two variants. The sweet *sanna* is made from jaggery and the plain savoury one is eaten as an accompaniment to curries or on its own.

Delicious *caldeirada* fish stew

9 Caldeirada

A cousin to the Greek *kakavia* and French *bouillabaisse*, this humble fishermen's stew uses a combination of lean and oily fish plus potatoes as a base, to give the dish a thick consistency. Shellfish and other seafood may be added along with vegetables.

10 Ambotik

True to its Konkani name (*ambot* means tangy and *tik* means spicy), this hot, sour and sweet fish curry is identified by its flaming orange colour due to the use of turmeric and Kashmiri chillies.

TOP 10 GOAN DRINKS

1 Feni
A famous local drink made from fermented cashew fruit or coconut sap, with a strong aftertaste.

2 Urrak
The cashew harvest season is the best time to sample this refreshing drink – a by-product of cashew-*feni* distillation.

3 Port Wine
Known for its distinctive fruity flavour, port wine is often enjoyed as a dessert wine or paired with cheese.

4 Sol Kadi
Kokum juice and coconut milk are combined with spices to create this drink, which is also a digestive aid.

5 Niro
Niro, or cashew juice, is best enjoyed locally from March to May.

6 Sula Wine
A popular Indian wine brand that offers a variety of red, white and rosé wines.

7 Piyush
A traditional Goan drink made from nutmeg, cardamom, buttermilk and *shrikhand*, a thick yogurt-based dessert.

8 Armada
The perfect cocktail base, this spiced liqueur is based on a centuries-old family recipe. It is the first Indian liqueur to win a Gold Outstanding award at the International Wine and Spirit Competition.

9 King's Beer
The distinctive lack of aftertaste and smooth texture makes this pilsner beer all the more light and refreshing.

10 Kokum Juice
This tangy drink, characterized by its deep-red colour, is made from *kokum* berries.

Refreshing *kokum* juice

🔟 Places to Eat

Laid-back interiors of Sublime

1 Sublime

Celebrity chef Chris Saleem Agha Bee is at the helm of this restaurant (see p95) in Assagao, which serves up flavours from around the world. Sample the fish carpaccio or ginger batter calamari. For mains, the Asiatic beef medallions with wasabi mash, the mega-organic salad or mustard-encrusted fish are good options.

2 Bomras

Chef Bawmra Jap's award-winning restaurant (see p95) is Goa's best-kept secret. Bomra's serves superb contemporary Burmese and Kachin cuisine in a relaxed chic garden setting. Try the aromatic-flavoured pickled tealeaf salad and the snapper with lemongrass and galangal. The mojitos and mouth-watering desserts on the menu are great as well.

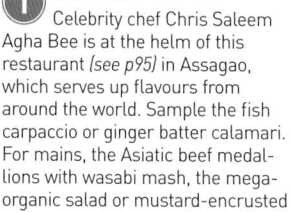

The dining area at Bomras

3 Thalassa

From ambience to food, this legendary open-air taverna (see p95) offers everything Greek. Diners swear by the Thalassa lobster platter. Apart from seafood, they also serve great desserts – try the baklava (sweet and syrupy layered filo-pastry) or the cheesecake. Book a table in advance to catch the sunset views.

4 The Black Sheep Bistro

A welcoming yellow façade gives way to elegant dark-wood interiors at this popular restaurant. Expect food that highlights fresh, local produce and goes well with their farm-to-table philosophy, promoting sustainable farming. While the red kismoor fish fillet is a favourite, there are many vegetarian options as well.

5 Sakana

Perfect for lovers of Japanese cuisine, Sakana (see p95) is situated near the red cliffs of Vagator Beach. Generous portions and a well-priced menu make it great value for money. Sushi, sashimi and salads are favourites. The menu features plenty of vegetarian options too.

6 A Reverie

Chic interiors, with a grand terracotta-tiled canopy and molecular gastronomy make this place extra special. The desserts are spectacular, a spin on classics such as cheesecake and banoffee pie.

7 Tamil Table

This beautiful courtyard restaurant *(see p95)* offers mouth-watering Chettinad dishes from Tamil Nadu and Puducherry. The in-house cocktails infused with spices are worth trying.

8 Baba Au Rhum

MAP H4 ▪ 1054, Sim Vaddo, Anjuna ▪ 0982 286 6366 ▪ ▨▨

Nestled in the quiet back roads between Anjuna and Baga, close to Bamboo Forest, Baba au Rhum has a casual and laid-back vibe. Enjoy comfort food at this café cum restaurant serving salads, burgers, thin-crust pizzas and more.

Alfresco dining at Baba Au Rhum

9 Ourem 88

British couple Jodie and Brett run this quaint garden restaurant *(see p103)*. The menu offers Euro gastro dishes created from fresh, local produce, such as beef Wellington, pork belly, calamari stuffed with chorizo and steaks are excellent. Try the chocolate fondant and cheesecake.

10 Hosa

A stylish restaurant *(see p95)*, located on the riverbank in Siolim, this place offers fusion south Indian tastes like curry leaf cured snapper and wild mushroom pongal. Be sure to try the chai inspired rum cocktail here.

TOP 10 BEACHFRONT RESTAURANTS

1 La Plage
MAP G3 ▪ 0982 212 1712 ▪ ₹₹
French-run eatery offering tuna with wasabi mash, pumpkin ravioli and a delicious chocolate *thali*.

2 Zeebop by the Sea
MAP D4 ▪ 0832 275 5333 ▪ ₹₹
This shack serves superb, fresh seafood. Do try the fish curry with rice and crab papadums.

3 Surya Beach Café
MAP D6 ▪ 0992 315 5396 ▪ ₹
Sample all kinds of seafood – oysters, mussels, crab, lobsters, clams – at this little-known beachside shack.

4 Zest Café
MAP D6 ▪ 88066 07919 ▪ ₹
This swanky beach café offers a healthy menu featuring raw desserts.

5 The Fisherman's Wharf
MAP D5 ▪ 0901 101 8866 ▪ ₹₹
Enjoy traditional Goan dishes such as prawn *balchao*, fish *reachado*, butter garlic prawns and crab curry at this legendary restaurant.

6 Dropadi Bar & Restaurant
MAP D6 ▪ 0832 264 4555 ▪ ₹₹
A mix of cuisines, with an emphasis on tandoori dishes are on offer here.

7 Slow Tide
MAP H4 ▪ 80552 55266 ▪ ₹₹₹
A New Age beach shack perched above Anjuna Beach, Slow Tide offers superb food and is known for its innovative and ingenious cocktails.

8 Burger Factory
MAP H3 ▪ 87886 30791 ▪ ₹₹
Arguably Goa's best burger joint, this place has quirky interiors and is famous for its gourmet burgers.

9 Pousada by the Beach
MAP H5 ▪ 0992 227 9265 ▪ ₹₹₹
Experience delectable Portuguese, Goan and Konkan cuisine at this laid-back beach shack.

10 Prana Mandrem
MAP H2 ▪ 0985 005 0403 ▪ ₹₹
Nutritious fare made from locally-sourced, fresh ingredients.

Fish tacos at Prana Mandrem

For a key to restaurant price ranges see p79

📶 Shops and Markets

A stall at the Goa Collective Bazaar

1 Goa Collective Bazaar

One of Goa's most popular night market's, the Goa Collective Bazaar (see pp14–15) takes place every Friday at HillTop (see p94). This vibrant night market is filled with colourful kiosks offering an array of items, such as apparel, jewellery, spices, handicrafts and souvenirs from all over India. The market aims to promote local artisans and designers by giving them a space to showcase their wares. There are quirky bars, food stalls and a stage featuring live music.

2 Velha Goa Galeria

Next door to the Panjim Inn (see p116), this store (see p78) specializes in exquisite traditional hand-painted azulejos, Portuguese tiles. The tiles are hand-painted by local artisans at the workshop in Aquem. Ceramic bowls, wall hangings, mirror frames and vases are also on sale here.

3 Anjuna Flea Market

The famous weekly flea market (see p15), held every Wednesday, takes place at the southern end of the beach. It has a range of stalls selling everything from silver jewellery and souvenirs to Rajasthani mirrorwork and Kerela woodcarvings. Trendy beachwear round off the selection, while added attractions include fortune-telling Nandi bulls. Prices are high, so be sure to haggle to pick up things at a reasonable rate.

4 Solar Souto Maior

Housed in a 16th-century palacio believed to be the only surviving mansion from Goa's "Golden Age", the Solar Souto Maior (see p78) boasts an art gallery and a museum shop, which sells antiques and collectibles. It also has a delightful garden café.

5 Vibrant Marché des Createurs

Inspired by the open-air bazaars of Morocco and the Middle East, this luxury market (see p93) has both local and international designer boutiques, housed in lavish tents.

6 Paper Boat Collective

One of Goa's most well-known boutiques, Paper Boat Collective (see p93) is housed in a beautiful 100-year-old Indo-Portuguese villa. It has a good collection of curated handcrafted products, ranging from ceramics and furniture to apparel.

Paper Boat Collective in Sangolda

Apparel and home decor at Rangeela

7 Rangeela

This trendy concept store *(see p93)* in Assagao is housed in an ancestral Goan villa. This is an ideal place to shop for contemporary fashion, souvenirs, accessories, jewellery and beachwear as well as beautiful textiles and home decor.

8 Artjuna

Set in an old Portuguese villa, surrounded by a pretty garden, this lifestyle boutique *(see p93)* boasts a great collection of handmade leather bags, jewellery, accessories, clothes and home decor. There's also a charming outdoor Mediterranean café with a kids' play area and a yoga *shala*.

9 Mapusa Market

Though the market *(see p15)* is open all days, Fridays are special as local vendors and traders sell fresh produce and a range of spices, Goan pottery and the spicy *chouriço* sausages in the covered colonnades in front of the rows of shops. In the lanes leading off from the main market are stalls selling handicrafts and souvenirs from all over the country.

10 The Attic

Collectors of antiques would not want to miss visiting The Attic *(see p93)*. It is known for its great collection of furniture and Goan antiques, which include intricate glassware as well as wooden chairs and candlesticks.

TOP 10 THINGS TO BUY

1 Azulejos
These beautiful Portuguese hand-painted tiles make a fine souvenir.

2 Bebinca
This traditional multi-layered dessert *(see p58)* of Portuguese origin is a treat worth buying to carry back.

3 Feni and Port Wine
The famous local speciality *feni* comes in cashew and coconut flavours. Another must-buy is the Goan port wine.

4 Spices
An essential ingredient in Goa's fiery cuisine, spices such as cardamom, clove and cinnamon are widely available.

5 Cashew nuts
Introduced by the Portuguese in Goa in around 1560, cashews are ubiquitous.

6 Pottery and Terracotta
Shop for statues of terracotta soldiers and cockerels that can be seen on the gates of traditional Goan houses, from Bicholim or Mapusa Market.

7 Jute Macramé
Buy jute lamp shades, flower pots and hangers at the boutiques in Goa.

8 Kunbi Saree
A cotton chequered saree *(see p90)* with a sturdy weave to withstand farming, it was worn by tribal women before the arrival of the Portuguese in Goa.

9 Chitari Woodcraft
The painted and lacquered furniture from the Chitari craftsmen in Cuncolim is worth looking out for.

10 Art and Antiques
Cartoonist Mario Miranda's sketches are available at galleries in Panaji and North Goa. Indo-Portuguese antiques and impressive hand-painted ceramics can be found in stores scattered across the state.

Ceramics at Velha Goa Galeria

Following pages Beautiful palm-fringed sandy Cola Beach

Goa for Free

The Church of St Cajetan in Old Goa

1 Old Goa

Located 10 km (7 miles) east of Panaji, Old Goa (see pp24–7) was built in the 15th century by the Adil Shahi dynasty of Bijapur. The port city was captured by the Portuguese in the early 16th century, but abandoned due to a plague in the 18th century. Today, the remains of the city are a UNESCO World Heritage Site.

Vibrant street art in Panaji

2 Street Art

Panaji features exciting street art that focuses on Goan culture. The walls of sombre grey buildings have been adorned with colourful murals and graffiti by the St+Art Goa Project as part of the annual Serendipity Arts Festival (see p69) with the aim of making art accessible to everyone. Don't miss US artist Miles Toland's "Fisher Woman" near Alfran Plaza.

3 Fort Aguada

Overlooking the Arabian Sea, the well-preserved Fort Aguada (see p12) was constructed to defend against attacks by the Marathas and Dutch. The fort got its name (aguada means water) from the freshwater spring within the fort that provided water to the ships that docked here.

4 Churches

Goa boasts some of the oldest churches in India and they showcase an amazing blend of Portuguese and Indian architecture. Among the more famous ones are the Basilica de Bom Jesus (see p24), Sé Cathedral (see p25), Church of St Francis of Assisi (see p24), Church of St Cajetan (see p25) and the Church of Our Lady of the Immaculate Conception (see p20).

5 Fontainhas

Cut off from Panaji's din, Fontainhas (see p20) is Goa's Latin Quarter. It offers a walk that is an experience in itself. The Portuguese influence is evident from the architecture. Look out for the narrow winding and tapered streets, flanked by old villas with tiled roofs and buildings painted in the traditional colours.

6 Goa Carnival

Celebrated since the 18th century, the boisterous Carnival (see p68) is Goa's most famous festival. It is believed that Goa comes under the rule of King Momo who encourages all to eat, drink and make merry.

7 Ferries

Goa has some of the best inland waterways, and ferry rides are a great way to admire the Goa skyline from the water. Most ferries operate daily and are free for foot passengers. Hop on a ferry from Querim to Tirakol or Old Goa to Divar Island, or catch the commuter ferry between Betim and Panaji.

8 Dudhsagar Falls

This four-tiered waterfall (see p32), among India's tallest, is located on the Mandovi. The best way to reach the falls is by car via Mollem. For those looking for more adventure, trekking is an option too.

9 Public Astronomical Observatory

Set up by the Association of Friends for Astronomy in 1990, the Public Astronomical Observatory (see p23) is an ideal place for amateur astronomers and stargazers. Owing to its seaside location and the lack of tall buildings, the view of the sky can be astounding. One can simply go for stargazing and beach astronomy, or attend the science film festival organized by the AFAO.

10 Mario Gallery

Discover how history shaped Goa through the years in signature Mario Miranda's style. His artworks are used on various articles such as crockery, T-shirts, postcards and illustrated books. These can be bought as souvenirs (see p16).

Souvenirs for sale at Mario Gallery

TOP 10 BUDGET TIPS

Motorbikes for hire

1 A convenient option for travelling around Goa is by gearless motorbikes, which can be rented easily (see p106).

2 Motorcycle rickshaws are a cheap mode of transport in Goa.

3 Skip conventional restaurants and try the beachfront restaurants (see p61) that Goa is famous for. They offer affordable and delicious food options that range from continental to local cuisine.

4 Various mobile apps offer online table reservation services plus discounts and cashbacks on restaurant bills. Dineout is a popular app that works for both Android and iOS. Set lunches and buffets as well as weekend brunches at popular restaurants can be very good value and cost less than the evening meals.

5 Many bars and pubs have "Ladies Nights" on weekdays where entry and drinks are free for women.

6 Most bars have happy hours during early evenings (usually 5–8pm) that offer "one plus one" on drinks as well as spirits.

7 Alcohol is cheaper in wine shops compared to in restaurants, bars or beach shacks.

8 Test your bargaining skills at local markets (see pp62–3) – you might get a good deal off the original quote.

9 Everything from room rates to food is cheaper during the off season months – April to October.

10 If you want to try your hand at gambling, visit the casinos on weekdays. The prices usually go up over the weekends from Friday to Sunday.

 Festivals

1 Three Kings Feast
6 Jan or first Sun in Jan

Grand processions take place at the Three Kings Church (see p97) during the *Festa dos Reis* (Three Kings Feast). Young boys from local villages re-enact the Three Magi blessing baby Jesus and are accompanied by crowds to Remedios Hill.

Church lit during Three Kings Feast

2 Shantadurga
Jan

During this famous festival, a silver statue of Hindu goddess Shantadurga (see p81) is carried in procession between the villages of Fatorpa and Cuncolim. It is also known as the "Procession of the Umbrellas", as it is led by 12 umbrellas, which represent different communities.

3 Goa Carnival
Pre-Lent

Goa's grandest festival is celebrated before Lent. It begins in Panaji with the crowning of King Momo, the king of chaos and fun. The parade has elaborate floats and masked revellers in fancy dress. Three days and nights of nonstop revelry follow, which ends at Vasco da Gama.

4 Shigmotsav (Shigmo)
Feb/Mar

A Goan rendition of the popular Hindu festival of colours, Holi, Shigmo features traditional folk dances and street floats depicting mythological and religious scenes. Highlights include the *Ghodemundi* during which men perform a martial dance with wooden horses strapped to the lower half of their bodies.

5 Sao Joao
Jun

This feast celebrates the arrival of the monsoon and honours the baptism of St John the Baptist. To mark this event, young people jump into lakes and ponds, and boat races are organized in Siolim (see p15).

6 Bonderam
Fourth Sat in Aug

The Bonderam festival takes its name from *bandeira*, which means flag in Portuguese. Held on Divar Island (see p82), it commemorates the Portuguese system of using flags to indicate property boundaries between feuding villagers. Mock

The colourful, festive annual Goa Carnival parade

Flag bearers at the start of Bonderam

fights are re-enacted to knock down the flags. Parties begin and bands strike up a tune from 7pm.

7 Narkasur Parades
Oct; Eve of Diwali

To celebrate the victory of the Hindu god Krishna over the demon Narkasur effigies of the demon are burned. This is meant to symbolize the victory of good over evil and heralds the festival of lights, Diwali.

8 Feast of St Francis Xavier
3 or 4 Dec

The feast of Goa's patron saint is held on the anniversary of his death. Attended by pilgrims from all over the world, the feast is preceded by *novenas* (nine days of prayer).

9 Feast of Our Lady of the Immaculate Conception
Early Dec

This holy feast is celebrated at the famous Church of Our Lady of the Immaculate Conception *(see p20)* to commemorate Mother Mary's conception. Festivities go on for a few days and street stalls are set up around the church. In the evening, there are firework displays.

10 Christmas and New Year
25 Dec–1 Jan

During the festive season, the streets and most churches across the state are beautifully decorated with lights. The Christmas eve Midnight Mass is traditionally known as *Misa de Galo*, (Cock's Crow) as it continues until dawn. On New Year's Eve, numerous beach parties are held accompanied by great firework displays.

TOP 10 MUSIC, CULTURAL AND ART FESTIVALS IN GOA

1 International Kite Festival
Two-day festival, including night kite flying at Miramar Beach (Jan).

2 Sensorium
Exhibition of arts, cinema and music at Sunaparanta, Goa Centre for the Arts (Jan–Mar, see p23).

3 Monte Music Festival
A cultural event for lovers of classical music and dance organized by Cidade de Goa and Fundação Oriente (Feb).

4 International Film Festival of India
India's largest film festival celebrates cinema by hosting screenings of Indian and international films (Nov).

5 Sunburn Festival
This popular three-day electronic dance music festival in Vagator features local and international artists (Dec).

6 Goa International Jazz Live Festival
Celebration of contemporary jazz showing performances by India's finest bands as well as international acts (Dec).

7 Serendipity Arts Festival
Multi-disciplinary event held at the Old Secretariat *(see p22)* on the banks of the Mandovi (Dec).

8 Goa Arts & Literary Festival (GALF)
Goa's literary and art festival features diverse writers, artists and musicians from all over the world (Dec).

9 Liberation Day
Military parades mark the liberation of Goa from Portuguese rule (17th Dec).

10 Zagor Festival
Siolim's main festival includes midnight processions bearing the effigy of the village deity Zagoryo, followed by a dance drama (Dec).

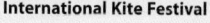

International Kite Festival

🔟 Excursions from Goa

Stunning waterfall in Amboli

1 Amboli
Maharashtra, 90 km (56 miles) from Panaji ■ Bus or car
Blessed with numerous waterfalls, this hill station is fondly called the "Queen of Maharashtra". A perfectly peaceful retreat, Amboli is among the world's top eco hotspots and is flush with unusual flora and fauna. Amboli Falls, Shirgaonkar Point, Madhavgad Fort and Hiranya Keshi Temple, are definitely worth a visit.

2 Chorla Ghat
Goa's hills (ghats) are just as beautiful as its beaches, with Chorla Ghat (see p84) being just one such example. Located on the Karnataka border in the Western Ghats, this area is ideal for jungle walks, treks and hikes.

3 Sawantvadi
Maharashtra, 62 km (39 miles) from Panaji ■ Train & bus
Located a short drive away from Panaji is the pretty little town of Sawantvadi. It has a palace named after the erstwhile rulers of the state, Khem Sawant. The current queen still lives in the palace with her family and promotes local arts such as woodwork painting. Workshops held in the palace attract locals and tourists. Moti Talao and Raghunath market merit a visit.

4 Dandeli
Maharashtra, 100 km (62 miles) from Panaji ■ Train & bus
An ideal place for outdoor enthusiasts, Dandeli has abundant wildlife and the sanctuary is home to diverse flora and fauna. Safaris, whitewater rafting, canoeing, kayaking, rappelling, mountain biking and trekking are some of the activities available here.

5 Hampi
Karnataka, 347 km (216 miles) from Panaji ■ Train & bus
A UNESCO World Heritage Site, Hampi is known for its architecture and history. Among the places

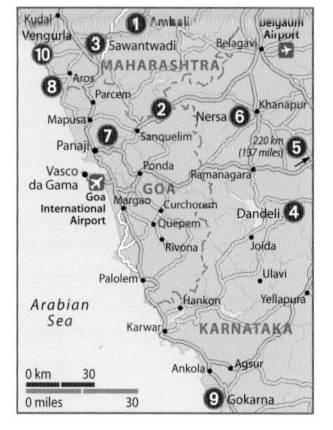

from Panaji, and Divar can be reached from Old Goa through short ferry rides. Go bird watching at the Salim Ali Bird Sanctuary *(see p84)*; walk or cycle through the picture perfect countryside dotted with elegant Portuguese villas and visit a small church at Divar.

8 Fort Tiracol
MAP G1 ■ 42 km (26 miles) from Panaji ■ Ferry from Querim

Once an armed fortress of the Portuguese, Fort Tiracol is now a heritage hotel *(see p121)* located on a cliff, offering breathtaking views of the Arabian Sea and Tiracol River.

to visit are the many temples, palace ruins, royal pavilions and ancient markets, along the Tungabhadra River, dating back to the Vijayanagara Empire.

6 Nersa
Karnataka, 113 km (70 miles) from Panaji ■ Train & bus

An off-the-beaten track village rich in biodiversity, Nersa is a haven for ornithologists. It is home to over 250 birds and 950 bat species. It is perfect for trekking too.

7 Chorão & Divar Islands
These two islands *(see p82)* are ideal to get a feel of rural Goa. Chorão Island can be accessed from Ribandar, a short drive away

Gigantic Shiva statue in Gokarna

9 Gokarna
Maharashtra, 164 km (102 miles) from Panaji ■ Car or bus

With its quiet beaches, beautiful temples and good food, Gokarna is a quaint town with a unique culture. Visit the iconic Om beach or Kudle, Paradise, Half Moon and Gokarna beaches. It is the perfect place for jet skiing, dolphin spotting, and fishing or simply for a stroll along the coast.

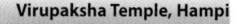

Virupaksha Temple, Hampi

10 Vengurla
Maharashtra, 65 km (70 miles) from Panaji ■ Train & bus

The charming town of Vengurla is known for its temples, rocks, white sand beaches, mango and cashew plantations and folk art known as Dashavtara. Watersports facilities are available and seafood is abundant.

Goa
Area by Area

**The enchanting Great Salon
of Braganza House**

🔟 Panaji and Old Goa

The Mandovi River serves as a beautiful backdrop to the current and former capitals of Goa, Panaji and Old Goa respectively. Full of colonial charm, Panjim – officially known by its Maharashtrian name Panaji, which means "land that does not flood" – retains an old-fashioned character, which is evident in its grand colonial era buildings and backstreets of the atmospheric Latin Quarter, Fontainhas. Linked to modern Panaji by a centuries-old causeway is Old Goa, once known as "Golden Goa" for its incredible prosperity. Foremost among the attractions here are its iconic Baroque churches, which have been classified as UNESCO World Heritage Sites. Nearby is lively Miramar Beach and quiet Dona Paula, replete with legends and known for its breathtaking sea views.

Statue at the Bishops Palace

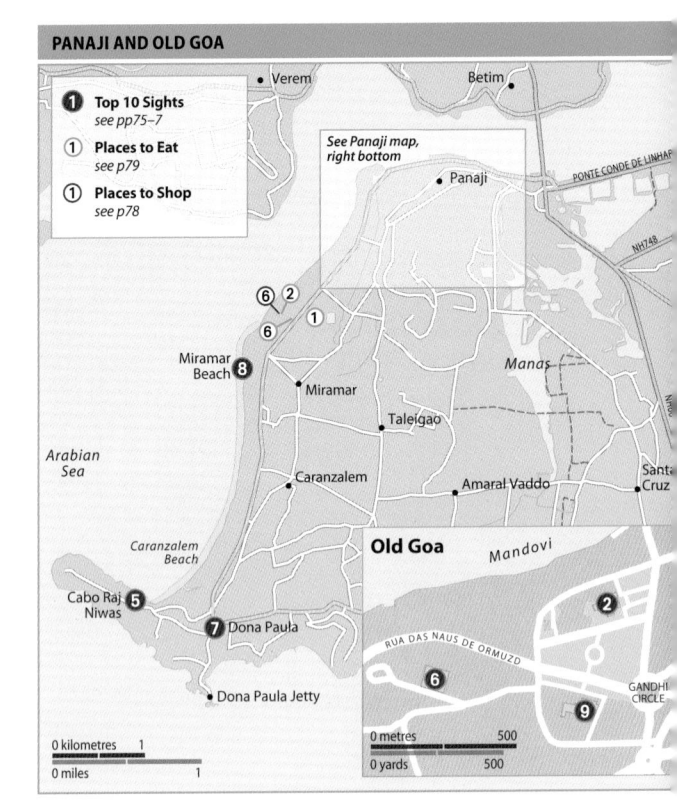

PANAJI AND OLD GOA

① Top 10 Sights
see pp75–7

① Places to Eat
see p79

① Places to Shop
see p78

See Panaji map, right bottom

Verem

Betim

Panaji

PONTE CONDE DE LINHARES

NH748

⑥ ②
⑥ ①

Miramar Beach ⑧

Miramar

Manas

Taleigao

Arabian Sea

Caranzalem

Amaral Vaddo

Santa Cruz

Caranzalem Beach

Cabo Raj Niwas ⑤

⑦ Dona Paula

Dona Paula Jetty

Old Goa

Mandovi

②

RUA DAS NAUS DE ORMUZD

⑥

GANDHI CIRCLE

⑨

0 kilometres   1
0 miles   1

0 metres   500
0 yards   500

1 Church of Our Lady of the Immaculate Conception

Overlooking Panaji's main square is the iconic Church of Our Lady of the Immaculate Conception *(see p20)*, built in 1541. The impressive double flight of stairs leading up to the church was added in 1871. The Baroque splendour of the main altar and the two transept altars is in sharp contrast to the otherwise simple interior.

Altar of a chapel at Sé Cathedral

2 Sé Cathedral

Ordered by the government in Portugal to build a church worthy of their mighty empire, Francis Coutinho (Viceroy, 1561–1564) envisaged a magnificent cathedral that would be the largest in Asia. The result is the Renaissance-style Sé Cathedral

(see p25). Its façade was flanked by two square bell towers, only one of which survives. In it hangs the Golden Bell, known for its melodic tones. The interior features a gilded high altar, dedicated to St Catherine of Alexandria, with panel paintings depicting scenes from her life.

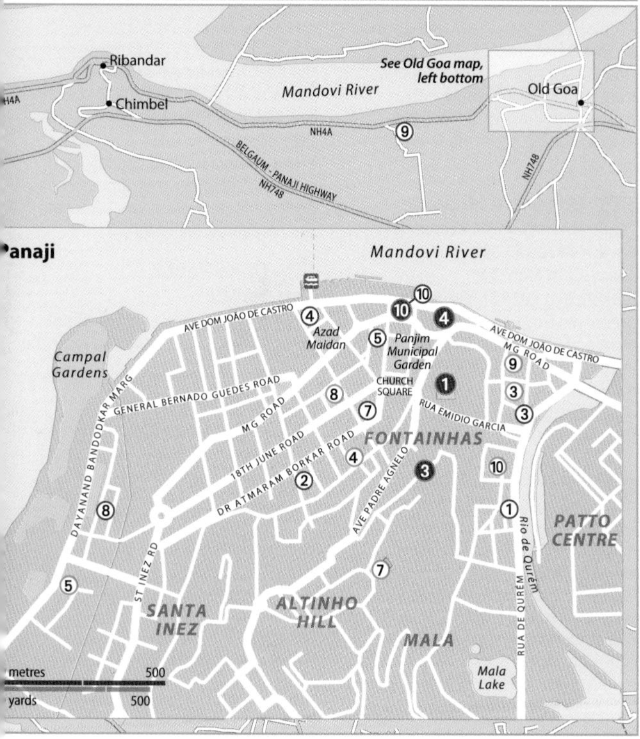

A street in Fontainhas flanked by brightly coloured Indo-Portuguese houses

③ Fontainhas

The capital's oldest and most colourful district, Fontainhas *(see p20)* is known for preserving the ambience of colonial times. Street names such as Rua 31 de Janeira (31st January Road) signify Portugal's independence from Spain, while 18th June Road commemorates the end of Portuguese rule in Goa. Look out for colour-washed houses and *azulejo* street signs.

④ Goa State Museum

MAP M2 ▪ EDC Complex, Patto ▪ 0832 243 8006 ▪ Open 10am–6pm Mon–Sat

Established in 1977, this museum preserves Goa's rich history. It houses a collection of pre-colonial artifacts, including statues, sati stones, carvings from ravaged Hindu temples, as well as some Christian icons. Look out for the furniture used by the Portuguese.

⑤ Cabo Raj Niwas

In 1760, this building *(see p22)* became the official residence of the viceroys – until 1918. Extensive renovations have transformed the original Islamic structure into the colonial building it is today, with a sloping tiled roof, wide wooden verandahs and cast-iron pillars. The Ashoka Chakra, the emblem of the Indian government, has replaced the Portuguese viceroys' coat of arms above the entrance.

⑥ Museum of Christian Art

MAP L6 ▪ Convent of Santa Monica, Velha Goa ▪ 0832 228 5299 ▪ Open 10am–4:30pm Mon–Sat

Asia's first Museum of Christian Art was established in 1991 by the Indian National Trust for Art and Cultural Heritage (INTACH) and the Gulbenkian Foundation of Portugal. The impressive collection includes 17th- and 18th-century religious objects such as silver and ivory ornaments, ornate clerical robes, processional crosses and holy water sprinklers.

⑦ Dona Paula

MAP D6

About 7 km (4 miles) southwest of Panaji, Dona Paula is located near the

---

THE GOAN INQUISITION

At the request of Francis Xavier, a tribunal of Jesuits arrived in 1560. Their mission was to curb the libertine ways of the Portuguese settlers and convert "infidels". Those who refused were locked away in the dungeons of the "Palace of the Inquisition" (as Adil Shah's palace was known) to await the *auto da fé* (acts of faith) trials. The condemned were burnt alive in front of a congregation of dignitaries. Over the next 200 years, 16,000 trials were held and thousands were killed, and it was not until 1812 that the Inquisition was finally dissolved.

headland dividing the estuaries of the Zuari and Mandovi rivers. According to legend, it is named after a viceroy's daughter who, it is believed, jumped into the sea when she wasn't allowed to marry a local fisherman. The jetty offers views of Fort Aguada, across the bay, and is especially beautiful during sunset. Jet skis are available for rent, and visitors can also take a ferry ride to Vasco da Gama harbour.

⑧ Miramar Beach
MAP K6

Panaji's nearest beach, Miramar is about 3 km (2 miles) west. Named Porta de Gaspar Dias by the Portuguese, this beach is a busy spot especially during the evenings. Several food trucks and shacks offer streetside snacks here.

Basilica de Bom Jesus in Old Goa

⑨ Basilica de Bom Jesus

Built by the Jesuits in 1594, this church (see pp24–7) is home to the world-famous mausoleum of Francis Xavier, Goa's patron saint.

⑩ Indian Customs & Central Excise Museum
MAP L1 ∎ Avenida Dom João de Castro, Ozari, Panaji ∎ 0982 366 5719 ∎ Open 9:30am–5pm Tue–Sun

Housed in a striking blue heritage building, this museum offers an insight into the history of the customs and excise departments in India. The museum has four galleries, which showcase an array of seized goods and antiques. On display are items such as the gilded idol of Jambala that was smuggled into India from Nepal.

A DAY IN PANAJI AND OLD GOA

▶ **MORNING**

A good way to get a feel of Goa's Portuguese ambience is by spending some time in Panaji, which is ideally located on the banks of the Mandovi River. Begin your morning with a cup of coffee at the **Caravela Café** (see p79) before heading to the nearby **Gallery Gitanjali** (see p20), an arts and cultural centre that displays works by national and international artists. Next, stop at the distinctive **Church of Our Lady of the Immaculate Conception** (see p75), an important landmark. Allow yourself an hour here. Then enjoy a riverside stroll along the Mandovi, passing attractions such as the **Old Secretariat** (see p22) and the striking **Statue of Abbé de Faria** (see p20) along the way. Next, enjoy a Goan fish *thali* for lunch at **Kokni Kanteen** (see p79).

AFTERNOON

After lunch, enjoy a drive along the Mandovi River to the Basilica de Bom Jesus and Sé Cathedral (see p75) in **Old Goa** (see pp24–7). The basilica is revered by Catholics from all over as it is home to the mortal remains of Goa's patron saint, Francis Xavier. It is advisable to dress conservatively when visiting. From Old Goa hop on board a bus to Panaji's Kadamba Bus Stand. Then take a short stroll back to the charming streets of Fontainhas, Goa's Latin Quarter. For dinner head to **Antonio@31** (see p79) in Fontainhas' Sao Tome neighbourhood to sample Goan tapas and delectable cocktails.

See map on pp74–5

Places to Shop

1 Velha Goa Galeria
MAP M2 ▪ Rua de Ourém, Panaji ▪ Open 10:30am–7:30pm Mon–Sat

An iconic store *(see p62)* in Goa's Latin Quarter, which specializes in traditional hand-painted *azulejos*.

2 Sacha's Shop
MAP L2 ▪ Swami Vivekananda Rd, Panaji ▪ 0832 222 2035 ▪ Open 10am–8pm Mon–Sat (from noon Sun)

Sacha Mendes's boutique has stylish Goan resort wear, statement jewellery, and bags. It also has designer labels.

3 Sosa's
MAP M2 ▪ E-245, Rua de Ourém, Panaji ▪ 0832 222 8063 ▪ Open 10:30am–7pm Mon–Sat

Shop for apparel by reputed designers such as Aki Narula, Rahul Mishra and Gaurav Gupta.

4 Aparant Goan Handicrafts Emporium
MAP L1 ▪ Crafts Complex, Malacca Rd, Panaji ▪ 0832 222 4478

This emporium promotes a variety of handicrafts such as woollen tapestries and carpets made by local artisans.

5 Mario Gallery
MAP L1 ▪ Below Aroma Hotel, Duarte Pacheco Rd, Panaji ▪ 0832 242 1776

Artworks of Goa's most celebrated artist, Mario Miranda, can be found here. The store offers various collectibles and his famous illustrations.

Prints for sale at Mario Gallery

6 Fabindia
MAP K2 ▪ Braganza House, C13/390, Campal, Panaji

This popular India-centric chain store is housed in the famous Braganza House *(see pp36–7)*. It is the perfect place to shop for clothes, furniture, organic food and natural cosmetics.

7 Khadi Gramodyog Bhavan
MAP L2 ▪ Municipality Building, Atmaram Borkar Rd, Panaji ▪ 0832 223 2746 ▪ Open 9am–7pm Mon–Fri

The Khadi and Village Industries Commission's emporium offers hand-made cottons, oils, soaps and spices.

8 Wendell Rodricks Design Space
MAP K2 ▪ 158, near Luis Gomes Garden, Panaji ▪ 0832 223 8177

The flagship store of designer Wendell Rodricks stocks an organic clothing line for men and women.

9 Solar Souto Maior
MAP M6 ▪ B-40, Maior Sao Pedro, Old Goa ▪ Open 9:30am–6:30pm daily

This heritage house *(see p62)* is an art gallery and a museum-shop displaying chandeliers, wall hangings and more.

10 Galeria Azujelos De Goa
MAP L1 ▪ Next to Sales Tax Office, Panaji ▪ 0982 297 6867 ▪ Open 10am–7pm Mon–Sat

Set inside Orlando de Noronha's 250-year-old home, this unique shop is ideal for gifts and souvenirs.

Places to Eat

PRICE CATEGORIES

For a meal for two, including taxes and service charge but not alcohol.

₹ under ₹1000 ₹₹ ₹1000–₹2000
₹₹₹ over ₹2000

 Mum's Kitchen
MAP J6 ▪ 854, Martins Building, D B St, Panaji ▪ 0982 217 5559 ▪ ₹₹₹

Dishes here are recreated from old family recipes collected from across the state. The *kombdechem sukhem* (spicy boneless chicken) is a speciality.

 **The Black Sheep Bistro**
MAP J6 ▪ Above Fabindia, Campal, Panaji ▪ 93250 23565 ▪ ₹₹₹

In BSB's *(see p60)* sophisticated dining room, a savvy take on globally inspired cuisine is the order of the day. Try their cocktails.

3 Antonio@31
MAP M2 ▪ 31st January Rd, Panaji ▪ 0838 005 7888 ▪ ₹₹

A friendly neighbourhood bar serving Goan inspired *tapas* and other small plates along with innovative cocktails.

4 Kokni Kanteen
MAP L3 ▪ Near Mahalaxmi Temple, Altinho, Panaji ▪ 0832 242 1972 ▪ ₹

This rustic restaurant serves coastal Konkani cuisine and hearty fish *thalis* (platters). There are plenty of vegetarian options too.

5 Cream Choc & Co
MAP J6 ▪ Dayanand Bandodkar Marg, Miramar, Panaji ▪ 0948 662 3749 ▪ ₹₹₹

A Goa-based artisanal chocolate boutique, Cream Choc & Co sells pralines, homemade gelato, chocolate bars and even some savoury treats.

6 Thai N Wok
MAP J6 ▪ Near Goa Marriot, Miramar ▪ 0832 246 1980 ▪ Open 11am–3pm & 7:30pm–2:30am ▪ ₹₹

Sample exceptional Thai and Pan-Asian cuisine at this wonderful fine dining restaurant. All dishes on the menu are made using fresh produce from its own farm.

7 Café Bodega
MAP L2 ▪ 63/C-8, Sunaparanta, Goa Centre for the Arts, Panaji ▪ 0832 242 1315 ▪ Closed Sun ▪ ₹₹

An alfresco café set in the courtyard of an art gallery, Café Bodega is the perfect spot to enjoy breakfast. The Vietnamese coffee is not to be missed.

The Black Sheep Bistro

8 Ritz Classic
MAP L2 ▪ 10678, 1st floor, Wagle Vision Building, 18th June Rd, Panaji ▪ 0832 242 6417 ▪ ₹

The flavour-packed food and competitive prices draw in a steady stream of diners through the day. Don't miss the fish *thali*.

9 Caravela Café
MAP M1 ▪ 27, 31st January Rd, Panaji ▪ 0832 223 7448 ▪ ₹₹

This quaint café serves delicious breakfast and light eats. The menu includes local specialities such as *rissois* (shrimp patties), chorizo *pao* (local bun), desserts and coffee.

10 Viva Panjim
MAP M2 ▪ Fontainhas, Panaji ▪ 0832 242 2405 ▪ ₹₹

Set in a converted 150-year-old heritage home, this lovely family-run restaurant tucked away in the back streets of Fontainhas truly is a hidden gem. The menu here offers traditional Goan specialities and excellent seafood dishes.

See map on pp74–5

🔟 Central Goa

Wedged between the Mandovi and Zuari rivers, Central Goa captivates with its cultural richness and exuberant landscape. From impressive waterfalls and wildlife sanctuaries to medieval temples and exotic spice farms, there are a wealth of options to explore here. The temples around Ponda draw pilgrims from all over while the islands of Chorão and Divar are rich with avifauna, offering an ideal setting for birdwatchers to explore the hinterlands of Goa.

Safa Shahouri Masjid, Ponda

① Ponda

Southeast of Panaji lies the main market town of Ponda *(see pp30–31)*. With the Portuguese expansion in Central Goa, over 550 temples were destroyed. Hindu priests fled with religious artifacts to regions that lay outside Portuguese control, especially the area around Ponda town, where they built new temples in the 17th and 18th centuries. These temples can be found in the forests around the town and are concentrated in two main clusters – the north and in the country-side, west of the town. Another main sight here is the Safa Shahouri Masjid.

CENTRAL GOA

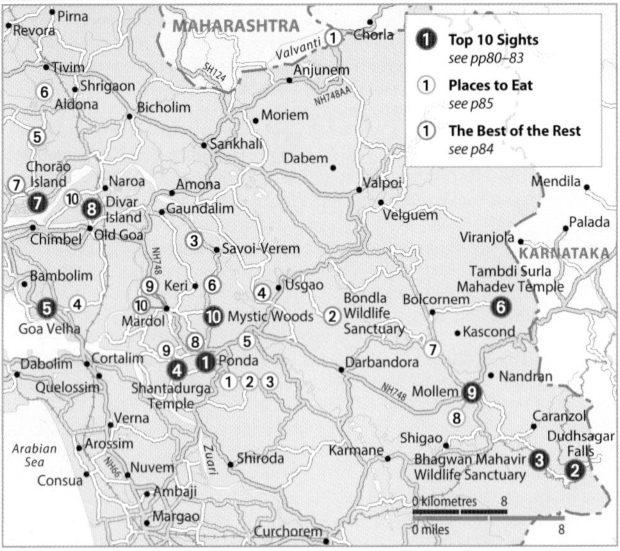

	Top 10 Sights
①	see pp80–83
①	**Places to Eat** see p85
①	**The Best of the Rest** see p84

Pirna
Revora
Tivim
Shrigaon ⑥
Aldona
⑤
MAHARASHTRA
Valvanti ① Chorla
Anjunem
Bicholim
SH124
NH748AA
Moriem
Sankhali
Dabem
Chorão ⑦ Island
Naroa
Amona
Valpoi
Mendila
⑦ ⑩ ⑧ Divar Island
Gaundalim
Velguem
Palada
Chimbel
Old Goa
③ Savoi-Verem
Viranjola
KARNATAKA
Bambolim
⑨ Keri ⑥
④ Usgao
Tambdi Surla Mahadev Temple
⑤ ④
Goa Velha
NH748
⑩ Mardol
⑩ Mystic Woods ② Wildlife Sanctuary
Bondla
Bolcornem
⑥
Kascond
Dabolim
Cortalim
⑧ ⑤
④ ① Ponda
① ② ③
Darbandora
⑦
Nandran
Quelossim
Shantadurga Temple
Verna
Shigao
NH748 Mollem ⑨
⑧
Caranzol
Dudhsagar Falls
Arabian Sea
Arossim
Nuvem
Consua
Zuari
Shiroda
Karmane
Bhagwan Mahavir Wildlife Sanctuary ③ ②
Ambaji
Margao
Curchorem
0 kilometres 8
0 miles 8

Goa's most impressive waterfall, Dudhsagar Falls

② Dudhsagar Falls

Set amid spectacular scenery with a pristine tropical forest as its backdrop, this 600-m-(1,969-ft-) high waterfall *(see p32)* on the Mandovi River is the main attraction on the Goa-Karnataka border. *Dudhsagar* is a Konkani name which means "sea of milk". It is derived from the clouds of foam that rise up as the water cascades down the rocky outcrop. To reach the waterfall, visitors can either hire a four-wheel-drive jeep or take the train to Colem and then trek to the base of the falls.

③ Bhagwan Mahavir Wildlife Sanctuary

The largest of Goa's four protected areas is the Bhagwan Mahavir Wildlife Sanctuary *(see p32)*. It is located 20 km (12 miles) southeast of Tamdi Surla and covers an area of 240 sq km (93 sq miles). The sanctuary is a paradise for birdwatchers and also features the Mollem National Park. Look out for the ruby-throated yellow bulbul here. Rich in wildlife, it is a good habitat for the *gaur* (Indian bison), spotted deer, hog, barking deer, leopards and elephants. The Devil's Canyon is a great viewpoint to spot wildlife. Visitors need a permit or an entry ticket to enter the sanctuary. It can be purchased at the park office.

④ Shantadurga Temple

MAP D3 ■ Kapileswari–Kavlem Rd, Donshiwado, Ponda ■ 0832 231 9900 ■ www.shreeshantadurga.com

About 3 km (2 miles) southwest of Ponda, at Kavlem, is the Shantadurga Temple *(see p45)*. Goa's most famous temple is dedicated to Shantadurga (also known as Santeri), who is the goddess of peace. The original temple was destroyed during the Portuguese rule, and a small mud shrine was built in its place. This was replaced by a European-inspired structure in 1730. Inside grand chandeliers hang from the gilded roof in the huge central hall. Also of interest is the golden *palkhi* (palanquin) in which the deity is carried during festive occasions.

Shantadurga Temple and the bell tower

5 Goa Velha

MAP C3

Also known as Gopakapttana, the Goa Velha village marks the site of Govapuri, the port-capital of the Kadamba rulers between the 11th and 13th centuries, of which few traces now remain. Every year on the first Monday of Easter week, the Procession of the Saints is held, when life-sized effigies of saints, martyrs, popes and cardinals are carried around the village. The celebrations end with a mass at St Andrews Church.

6 Tambdi Surla Mahadev Temple

This ancient temple *(see p33)*, hidden away in the forests of Tambdi Surla, dates from the Kadamba period (between the 11th and 13th centuries). Dedicated to Mahadeva (Shiva), the temple has an entrance hall with ten pillars, and the *shikhara* (spire) above the sanctum has a miniature relief and fine carvings of Brahma, Vishnu, Shiva and his consort, Parvati.

7 Chorão Island

MAP L5

The picturesque island of Chorão *(see p71)* can be reached by ferry from Ribandar, which is about 5 km (3 miles) east of Panaji. It is also known as Ilha do Fidalgos or "Island of Nobelmen" after the Portuguese. The island is home to the Salim Ali Bird Sanctuary *(see p84)*, which is considered a bird-watchers paradise. Fringed by mangrove swamps, the sanctuary has flying foxes and several different species of coastal birds. The brown mudflats are also a good place to spot the bulbous-headed mudskipper.

8 Divar Island

MAP L5

This is a great place to experience the untouched landscape of Goa. Isolated from the mainland and accessible only by ferry from Old Goa, Divar Island *(see p71)* was once an important religious centre in pre-colonial Goa. Divar derives it name from the Konkani *dev*, which translates to "god", and *vaddi* to "place". The two main areas on the island, Piedade and Malar, are best

Kadamba-period Tambdi Surla Temple

explored on a bike. The Church of Our Lady of Compassion occupies a hilltop in Piedade. Visitors can enjoy superb views of Old Goa from here.

Bonnet macaque, Mollem National Park

9 Mollem

Located on the foothills of the Sahyadri Mountain range, this small village *(see pp32–3)* serves as the main entry point for the Bhagwan Mahavir Wildlife Sanctuary. Visitors can also access Mollem National Park, which covers an area of 107 sq km (41 sq miles). The nearest railhead, Colem (Kulem) is 5 km (3 miles) south and is a drop-off point for Dudhsagar Falls.

10 Mystic Woods

This unique conservatory *(see p30)* has been designed by Jyoti and Yashodhan Heblekar as a sanctuary for the study and conservation of butterflies. Once a barren hill slope, this area now features plenty of flora and hundreds of species of colourful butterflies, all out in the open. The best time to visit is from 9am to noon, and August to November is when you can spot the most butterflies. There's also a spice farm which focuses on natural farming techniques. Another highlight is the fossil museum, which has Goa's best private collection of geodes and fossils.

A DAY IN CENTRAL GOA

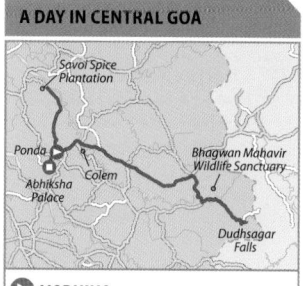

▶ MORNING

Brace yourself for a busy day packed with outdoor activities. Before you set out, it is advisable to book a taxi for the entire day. Start early as from **Ponda** *(see p80)*, it's a one-hour-long drive to the village of **Colem** *(see p33)*. From Colem hire a four-wheel-drive jeep, which will take you on a bumpy 45-minute ride through the **Bhagwan Mahavir Wildlife Sanctuary** *(see p81)* en route to the famous **Dudhsagar Falls** *(see p81)*. The drive ends with an enjoyable 15-minute hike to the base of the falls. For the adventurous, it is possible to trek to Dudhsagar as there is a 11-km- (7-mile-) long trail from Colem. On reaching the falls, enjoy a swim in the refreshing waters of India's second highest waterfall. Look out for monkeys that frequent the area. Remember to carry food and water as there are no shops in the vicinity of the falls. By noon, begin heading back to Colem by jeep.

AFTERNOON

From here head to the **Savoi Spice Plantation** *(see p30)* in Ponda, which is about an hour-long drive away. Take a one-hour guided tour of the 40-ha (100-acre) plantation. The cashew distillation unit here is an added attraction. The tour is followed by lunch, usually a *thali* of Goan specialities. Note that the plantation does not require advance booking and tickets can be bought on arrival. If you have the time and inclination to shop for souvenirs, head to the local market, before enjoying dinner at **Abhiksha Palace** *(see p85)* in Ponda.

See map on p80 ←

The Best of the Rest

① Chorla Ghat
MAP E1 ▪ 50 km (31 miles) NE of Panaji ▪ Bus or car

Part of the Western Ghats, in the Sahyadri Mountain range, the Chorla Ghat *(see p70)* is at an elevation of 800 m (2,625 ft). It is ideal for hiking and birdwatching.

Malabar giant squirrel at Bondla's sanctuary

② Bondla Wildlife Sanctuary
MAP E3 ▪ Khandepar Belgaum Rd, Ponda ▪ 0992 374 9287 ▪ Adm

Spot animals such as the sambar deer, Malabar giant squirrel, Indian peafowl and many more here. This sanctuary is known for its successful breeding of the *gaur* (Indian bison). There's also a lovely botanical garden and library.

③ Mahalasa Temple
The temple's *(see p31)* entrance porches have carvings of musicians and warriors. The most distinguishing feature here is an exceptionally tall brass pillar with 21 tiers in all.

④ Caves of Khandepar
About 4 km (2 miles) northeast of Ponda, near the village of Khandepar on the banks of the river, is a cluster of Hindu rock-cut caves *(see p31)*. Take note of the striking lotus decorations on the ceiling.

⑤ Olaulim Backyards
MAP C3 ▪ Olaulim, Aldona ▪ 98233 90233

A beautiful inland resort with four eco-friendly cottages set on the backwaters of the Mandovi River. It's a quiet, peaceful retreat offering kayaking, nature trails and a pool.

⑥ Tropical Spice Plantation
North of Ponda, this popular plantation *(see p30)* organizes guided tours to show visitors how spices are produced.

⑦ Salim Ali Bird Sanctuary
MAP K5 ▪ Chorão Island, Ribandar ▪ 0832 222 8772 ▪ Open 6am–6pm daily ▪ Adm

Immensely popular with locals and tourists, this mangrove habitat *(see p82)* is also a birdwatchers paradise.

⑧ Safa Shahouri Masjid
Little remains of the former grandeur of Goa's oldest remaining mosque *(see p31)*. Its exterior has a distinctive green dome, elegant Islamic arches and octagonal pillars.

⑨ Savoi Spice Plantation
A one-hour guided tour of this plantation *(see p30)* is followed by lunch, usually a *thali* of Goan specialities. Local crafts items are sold here.

⑩ Shri Mangueshi Temple
MAP D3 ▪ Dinanath Mangeshkar Rd, Mardol ▪ Open 6am–10pm

Goa's wealthiest temple *(see p45)*, dedicated to Shiva, is one of the most frequently visited temples in the state. Dance-dramas are performed here during the *jatra* festivities.

Shri Mangueshi Temple, Mardol

Places to Eat

PRICE CATEGORIES
For a meal for two, including taxes and
service charge but not alcohol.

₹ under ₹1000 ₹₹ ₹1000–₹2000
₹₹₹ over ₹2000

1 Café Bhonsle
MAP D3 ■ Royal Building,
Kasiwada ■ 0832 231 8725 ■ ₹

Enjoy a hearty meal at Café
Bhonsle, which has many branches
throughout the state. This vegetarian restaurant offers a range of
Goan specialities.

2 Dee Sigdii House
MAP D3 ■ Shanti Nagar, Ponda
■ 0832 231 8700 ■ Closed D Mon ■ ₹

A casual eatery with cosy wooden
interiors. Fresh seafood dishes
dominate the menu. The tandoori prawns are a favourite.

3 Abhiksha Palace
MAP D3 ■ First floor, Tiska
■ 0907 599 2827 ■ ₹

This pocket-friendly
restaurant in Ponda
has outdoor seating
on its terrace. The food
is delicious and the por-
tions are generous.
Try the apple chicken.

4 Mom's Recipes
MAP C3 ■ Pilar, opposite Heritage
Centre, Goa Velha ■ 90217 64151
■ Open noon–3pm & 7–11pm Mon–
Wed & Fri–Sun ■ ₹₹

Mouthwatering Goan fish *thali* is the
speciality at the small, family-run
Mom's Recipes.

5 Sahakari Spice Farm
MAP D3 ■ Ponda Belgaum
Highway, Curti ■ 0832 231 4166
■ Closed D ■ ₹₹

Sample a traditional Goan lunch at
this farm *(see p31)*. Cooked in earthen
pots and served on a banana leaf,

the thali with Goan specialities
is wholesome. Round off the meal
with the local drink, *feni*.

6 Okapi Vegan Kitchen
MAP C2 ■ Quitula, Aldona
■ 098208 16965 ■ Open noon–
3:30pm Mon & Wed–Fri, 5–10:30pm
Sat & Sun ■ ₹₹

A beautiful vegan café in the pretty
village of Aldona, this place is known
for its delicious plant-based food
and amazing in-house bakery. Look
out for cooking workshops, which
are run sporadically.

7 Nature's Nest
MAP E3 ■ Surla, Sancordem
■ 0840 795 4664 ■ ₹₹

Close to Dudhsagar Falls *(see p32)*,
this relatively remote restaurant
is in a resort. Diners can enjoy
mouthwatering Goan delica-
cies in a wonderful setting.

8 Karibu Garden
MAP F3 ■ Collem Rd,
Mollem ■ 0942 381 4466
■ ₹₹

A perfect pitstop on the
way to Dudhsagar Falls
(see p32), this place serves
Goan specialities as well as
Chinese cuisine.

**Fried pomfret with
rice and vegetables**

9 Tilve
MAP D3 ■ NH 17B,
Donshiwado ■ 0982 322
4545 ■ ₹₹

A family-run restaurant, Tilve
focuses on homemade traditional
seafood. Enjoy the fried pomfret or
the prawn fry. The menu offers
plenty of vegetarian options as well.

10 Island House
MAP L5 ■ No. 45 Goltim, Divar
Island ■ 082982 92257 ■ ₹₹

Tucked away on picturesque Divar
Island, Island House is a gorgeous
villa with a lovely restaurant that
offers superb Goan meals and
Kerala cuisine.

See map on p80

TOP 10 North Goa

A breathtaking coastline with a series of lovely beaches, North Goa is a sunseeker's paradise. The busy strip stretching from Candolim all the way to Arambol features a string of enduringly popular places to eat, lively bars, yoga retreats, an eclectic flea market, a vibrant night bazaar and exciting watersport options. Away from the sands, fascinating museums such as the Museum of Goa and the picturesque villages of Siolim and Assagao await exploration. It's little wonder that North Goa is a firm favourite with visitors.

A Pepper Cross at MOG

NORTH GOA

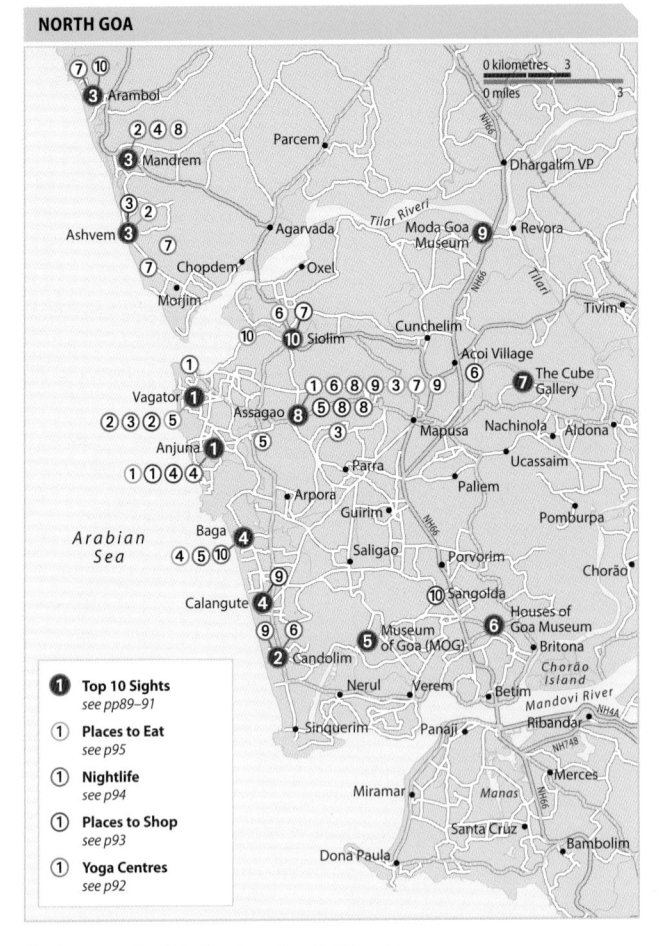

- **1** Top 10 Sights
  see pp89–91
- **1** Places to Eat
  see p95
- **1** Nightlife
  see p94
- **1** Places to Shop
  see p93
- **1** Yoga Centres
  see p92

Previous pages Candolim Beach seen from Fort Aguada

Sandy Vagator Beach fringed with coconut palms

1 Vagator and Anjuna

With red stone cliffs and the ramparts of the crumbling Chapora Fort soaring above it, Vagator (see p46) is a prime spot with a number of hotels, clubs and restaurants. A little towards the south is where the cove of Little Vagator (or Ozran) lies below a steep cliff, where a fresh-water stream empties into a clear pool, ideal for swimming. A short distance away is Anjuna, which is sprinkled with cafés, yoga retreats, guesthouses and bars. It also offers watersports such as jetskiing and paragliding. The popular Anjuna Flea Market (see p93), held every Wednesday, is crowded with hawkers from all over India (see pp14–15).

2 Candolim

Apart from its bustling beach, which stretches right up to Fort Aguada (see p12), Candolim also features other places of interest. The highlight here is the fort, which was built in 1612 to protect the northern shores of the Mandovi from the Dutch and Maratha invaders. Visitors can enjoy panoramic views from its four-storey Portuguese lighthouse. Candolim has numerous beach cafés. Several popular local restaurants also line the busy Fort Aguada Road.

3 Ashvem, Mandrem and Arambol

Ashvem is the perfect place to enjoy a swim, indulge in fine dining and experience Goan nightlife. Mandrem and Arambol are among the many fishing villages along the northern coastline. A quiet village with a lovely wide beach, Mandrem is the quietest of the beaches on this stretch. It is a great place for yoga and, when the wind picks up, kitesurfing. Nearby, Arambol, also known as Harmal, has an energetic vibe. There's a sunset point on the beach as well, which is lively in the evenings with drum circles and travellers practising tai chi and capoeira.

4 Calangute and Baga

Both Calangute and Baga (see pp16–17) are home to the state's busiest beaches. A string of eateries and shops line both beaches. The nightlife is mainly centred around Baga and the various clubs and bars along Tito's Lane. Visitors can choose from a wide range of watersport activities that are on offer at both beaches.

Fort Aguada Lighthouse, Candolim

Exhibit at the Museum of Goa

5 Museum of Goa (MOG)

Founded by artist Subodh Kerkar *(see p43)*, this museum *(see p13)* is spread across three floors covering 1,500 sq m (16,146 sq ft). The gallery space features various art forms such as sculptures, paintings, photography, installations and moving images. Much of the art is influenced by Goa's history and interactions with the spice route. Look out for the giant sized artistic rendition of chillies. The studio as well as its landscaped surroundings serve as display areas.

6 Houses of Goa Museum

A quirky triangular-shaped structure, the Houses of Goa Museum *(see p13)*, aims to showcase Goan architectural traditions. Built by local architect Gerard da Cunha, this unique museum traces the history and impact of Portuguese influences

An altar at the Houses of Goa Museum

KUNBI SAREE

This traditional saree *(see p63)* was worn by women from the Kunbi tribe, one of the oldest tribes of Goa who were paddy field workers, before the arrival of the Portuguese. It is dyed in red and black and woven in small and large checks. Designer Wendell Rodricks has received praise for reviving the weaving of this saree and helping restore its lost glory.

on Goan architecture, by highlighting the changes in decor and style of residential houses.

7 The Cube Gallery

MAP K4 ▪ 430/1 Calizor Vaddo, Moira ▪ 0942 280 6748 ▪ Open 11am–6pm Wed–Sun ▪ Adm

A contemporary arts space, The Cube Gallery is based in the village of Moira. Designed by Satinder "Sonny" Singh and his wife Carolina Paez, this gallery offers a fascinating visual experience. Cubes form the basis of the gallery's architecture, and the recessed lighting and elegant landscaping make for an extraordinary spectacle at night. There's a terrace garden and a lawn with life-size sculptures.

8 Assagao

Between Mapusa and Anjuna lies the quiet and beautiful Assagao *(see p15)*, which makes for a pleasant stay. This village, known for its yoga retreats, whitewashed churches and Portuguese villas, is ideally located a short distance away from Goa's frenetic beachside energy. Assagao's

culinary reputation continues to grow with the increase in its dining options, which include outdoor restaurants.

9 Moda Goa Museum

MAP C2 ▪ 515, St Anthony Waddo ▪ 0832 242 0604 ▪ Open 10am–6pm daily ▪ Adm

Famous Goan fashion designer Wendell Rodricks (see p43) has converted his 450-year-old villa, Casa Dona Maria, in Colvale into India's first museum of fashion. This one-of-a-kind museum is dedicated to documenting and tracing the rich history and lineage of costumes in Goa. There are 15 galleries, which feature exhibits such as sculptures, paintings, illustrations, clothing, accessories, jewellery and photographs. The museum plans to introduce research rooms to feature textiles and embroideries from all over India.

A Portuguese mansion in Siolim

10 Siolim

One of Goa's most charming villages, Siolim (see p15) offers a peaceful stay due to its location inland away from the state's nearest beaches on the northern coastline. The beautiful colonial era mansions here exude an air of Portuguese prosperity. The village is home to the Corinthian Church of St Anthony, one of the oldest Christian shrines in the region. The church is known for two miracles, which were witnessed by the entire congregation in the 16th-century.

A DAY IN NORTH GOA

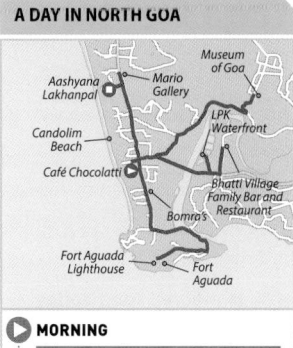

► MORNING

Begin the day with a typical English breakfast at the delightful **Café Chocolatti** (Map J6; 409A, Fort Aguada Rd, Candolim; open 9am–7pm Mon–Sat). Be sure to try their brownies and Belgian-style chocolate truffles as well. Next, take a stroll to **Candolim Beach** (see p12) where you can simply relax under a parasol or opt for watersports such as waterskiing or parasailing. Then, make a quick trip to the **Mario Gallery** (see p16) to shop for Mario Miranda's sketches of Goan life, which are perfect souvenirs and keepsakes. From here take an autorickshaw to bustling Fort Aguada Road for an exceptional lunch of contemporary Burmese cuisine at **Bomra's** (see p60).

AFTERNOON

Candolim Beach stretches all the way to your next stop, **Fort Aguada** (see p12), which is set on a hilltop. To enjoy the views, climb to the top of the **Fort Aguada Lighthouse** (see p12), which overlooks the vast expanse of sand and sea. Spend an hour here before taking a 25-minute taxi ride to Pilerne to explore the **Museum of Goa** (see p13). Later in the evening, stop at **Bhatti Village Family Bar and Restaurant** (Bhatti Waddo, Nerul; 0982 218 4103) for authentic Goan food before taking a stroll down to **LPK Waterfront** (see p57) for a night of dancing. End the day by staying overnight in one of the cottages at **Aashyana Lakhanpal** (see p116).

See map on p88

Yoga Centres

1 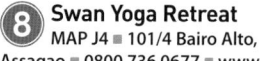 **Purple Valley Centre**
MAP J4 ■ H. No. 142, Bairo Alto, Assagao ■ 0832 226 8364
■ www.yogagoa.com

A tranquil yoga *shala*, Purple Valley offers accommodation that ranges from simple cottages, to luxurious houses. Healthy meals are served on the terrace.

2 **Himalaya Yoga Valley**
MAP G2 ■ Mandrem Beach, Junas Wadda ■ 0703 830 6467
■ www.yogagoaindia.com

India's premier yoga education centre offers training courses for both beginners as well as seasoned practitioners.

3 **Satsanga Retreat**
MAP J4 ■ Naika Vado, Parra
■ 0982 213 5009 ■ www.satsanga retreat.com

This retreat describes itself as a "home away from home". It offers training as well as workshops for yoga teachers.

A yoga class at Satsanga Retreat

4 **Ashiyana Yoga Centre**

This riverside tropical retreat *(see p18)* offers a long list of yoga courses from October to April. The on-site accommodation features heritage rooms and huts.

5 **Brahmani Yoga Centre**
MAP H4 ■ Tito's White House, Anjuna ■ 0937 056 8639 ■ www.brahmaniyoga.com

Established in 2003 by Julie Martin, who initiated Brahmani Yoga, this

is an internationally acclaimed yoga centre. It offers drop-in yoga classes that are conducted by expert teachers.

6 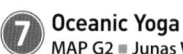 **Shala 142**
MAP J4 ■ Bairo Alto, Assagao
■ 9765 760 691

This yoga studio in Assagao provides a serene space for yoga, movement, music and therapy. Some of the yoga classes are drop-ins.

7 **Oceanic Yoga**
MAP G2 ■ Junas Wada, Mandrem Beach ■ 0904 924 7422
■ www.oceanicyoga.com

The founder of this centre, Yogi Abhay, has meticulously fine-tuned the training courses to teach the practical and theoretical aspects of yoga.

8 **Swan Yoga Retreat**
MAP J4 ■ 101/4 Bairo Alto, Assagao ■ 0800 736 0677 ■ www.swan-yoga-goa.com

Set in a peaceful corner of Assagao, this retreat offers a Zen yoga experi-ence in the *satyananda* and *hatha* tradition. Accommodation and meals are provided for week-long stays.

9 **Mojigao**
MAP J4 ■ Bairo Alto, near Ganga Tiles, Assagao ■ 0772 208 1090 ■ www.mojigao.com

Several holistic and wellness workshops are offered at this popular centre, including yoga and meditation classes, held daily at the lovely open-air yoga *shala*, surrounded by lush forests and hills.

10 **Himalayan Iyengar Yoga Centre**
MAP G2 ■ Madhlo Vaddo, Arambol
■ 0981 661 1075 ■ www.hiyoga centre.com

Founded in 1985 by Anand Sagar, this centre offers a number of yoga and meditation courses, including yoga for kids.

See map on p88

Places to Shop

Colourful items at Anjuna Flea Market

1 Anjuna Flea Market
A riot of colours, stalls and goods greet shoppers at this overwhelmingly popular market (see p62).

2 Goa Collective Bazaar
MAP H4 ▪ Hill Top, Vagator ▪ Open 5pm–midnight Fri
Shop for trinkets, sample local food and enjoy live music at this fun Friday night bazaar (see p62).

3 Vibrant Marché des Créateurs
MAP G3 ▪ Ashvem Beach (behind La Plage) ▪ Open daily ▪ www.vibrant-marche-des-createurs.business.site
Goa's first luxury market (see p62) is open daily. It focuses on clothing by top national and international designers.

4 Artjuna
MAP H4 ▪ 972 Market Rd, Monteiro Vaddo, Anjuna ▪ Open 8am–7:30pm daily
This trendy boutique (see p63) has a Mediterranean café. It stocks women's clothing, accessories and homeware.

5 Rangeela
MAP H4 ▪ Saunta Vaddo, Assagao ▪ Open 10am–9:30pm daily ▪ www.rangeelagoa.com
Set in quiet Assagao, this store (see p63) is housed in a lovingly restored old Goan mansion. It sells souvenirs, jewellery, clothes, decor, furniture and more.

6 The Attic
MAP J4 ▪ H. No. 69, near Mount Carmel Chapel Camarcazana, Mapusa ▪ Open 10am–7pm Mon–Sat
A stylish, contemporary gallery, The Attic (see p63) features exquisite vintage furniture and intricate glassware.

7 Karma Collection
MAP J3 ▪ 39 Duler-Marna-Siolim Rd, Siolim ▪ 0989 036 2659
A treasure trove of vintage textiles, furniture and collectibles, Karma Collection is located in a pretty house near St Anthony's Church in Siolim.

8 The Flame Store
MAP J5 ▪ 41, Saunta Vaddo, opposite Rangeela, Assagao▪ Open 11am–9:30pm daily
Housed in a beautifully restored Goan villa, this chic store features an eclectic collection of jewellery, accessories and luxury clothing by local and international designers.

9 Literati
Set in the midst of a large garden is a treasure trove of books. This 100-year old bookshop (see p17) has a lovely reading room and a café.

10 Paper Boat Collective
MAP J5 ▪ 248, Bella Vista, Chogm Rd, Sangolda ▪ Open 10:30am–7:30pm Mon–Sat
This concept store (see p62) is an ideal place to shop for latest items exclusively created by Indian designers.

Cosy interior of Paper Boat Collective

Nightlife

 House of Chapora
MAP H3 ■ Chapora Jetty, H.No 340/2 Village Anjuna-Caisua ■ 7448234869 ■ Open 11am–11:30pm Mon–Fri, 1am–midnight Sat & Sun

Whether you want to grab a sundowner or a fun night of music and dance, House of Chapora is the ideal spot for partygoers.

2 HillTop
MAP H4 ■ Ozran Beach Rd, Vagator ■ 0703 806 6665 ■ Open winters only: Nov–Mar ■ www.hilltopgoa.in

Goa's iconic party destination, HillTop (see p56) attracts visitors from across the globe.

3 Hideaway Café and Bar
MAP H4 ■ Near HillTop, Ozran Beach Rd, Vagator ■ 8605 219 351

This is a great place to visit if you are looking for live music, good service, tasty food and affordable drinks.

4 Shiva Valley
MAP H4 ■ Anjuna Beach, near Anjuna Flea Market ■ 0968 962 8008 ■ Open 9am–11pm daily

Known for its psychedelic parties, Shiva Valley (see p57) is popular for its cutting-edge music.

5 Club Tito's
MAP H5 ■ Titos Lane, Baga ■ Open 9am–3am Tue–Sun ■ www.titosgoa.com

One of the first clubs to open in Goa, this spot (see p56) has achieved legendary status.

6 Sinq Night Club
MAP H5 ■ Opposite Taj Holiday Village, Aguada Rd, Candolim ■ Open 10pm–3am daily ■ www.sinq.in

An upbeat and trendy club (see p56) which offers great entertainment.

7 Ecstatic Dance Shunya
MAP G2 ■ 215, Shunya Wellness, Arambol ■ 0991 117 9996 ■ Opening times vary, call ahead

This international dance community hosts Ecstatic (or free form) dance events twice a week with resident and guest DJs from all over the world.

8 Mojigao
MAP H4 ■ Bairo Alto, Assagao ■ 0982 353 9000 ■ www.mojigao.com

The beautiful jungle-themed restaurant at Mojigao hosts live trance music on full moon nights.

9 Cohiba
MAP J6 ■ Aguada–Siolim Rd, Aguada Fort Area, Candolim ■ 0772 203 1222 ■ Open 6pm–2am daily

Close to the Aguada Fort Lighthouse (see p12), this club has a welcoming vibe. The foot-stomping music is great.

10 Cape Town Café
MAP H5 ■ Tito's Lane, Baga Calangute Rd ■ 0992 332 5638 ■ Open 6pm–4am daily

Hosting international DJs, this place entertains its guests well. Watch live sporting events on its LCD screens.

Partygoers at Club Tito's

Places to Eat

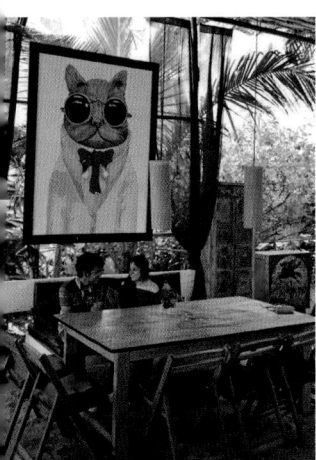

Outdoor seating at Bomras

1 Bomras
MAP H4 ■ Mazal Waddo, Anjuna ■ 0976 759 1056 ■ ₹₹₹

This award-winning Burmese restaurant *(see p60)* is known for its mouthwatering fare.

2 La Plage
MAP H3 ■ Ashvem Beach, Morjim ■ 9822 121 712 ■ ₹₹₹

Enjoy classic French dishes, superb beach views and a lovely ambience at this romantic restaurant located on a secluded beach.

3 Sublime
MAP H3 ■ H.No 481, Bouta Waddo, Assagao ■ 0982 248 4051 ■ Closed Tue ■ ₹₹₹

Set in a beautiful Portuguese villa, this restaurant focuses on contemporary fusion food made using fresh, organic produce.

4 Brittos
MAP J4 ■ Saunto Vaddo, Baga ■ 703 868 7292 ■ ₹₹

This legendary shack has a great location by the beach. It serves exceptional crab masala, fish curry and delicious calamari *vindaloo*.

PRICE CATEGORIES
For a meal for two, including taxes and service charge but not alcohol.

₹ under ₹1000 ₹₹ ₹1000–₹2000
₹₹₹ over ₹2000

5 Sakana
MAP H4 ■ Chapora Rd, Vagator ■ 0989 013 5502 ■ ₹₹₹

Owned by a Japanese-Israeli couple, Sakana is one of the few Japanese restaurants in Goa. The menu features sushi, udon noodles, salmon rolls and chicken katsu.

6 Hosa
MAP H3 ■ Near St Anthony's Church, Siolim ■ 0749 862 7977 ■ ₹₹

A stunning restaurant with chic decor specializing in fusion food and infused cocktails.

7 Avo's Kitchen
MAP J4 ■ Saunta Vardi, Assagao ■ 0951 830 5003 ■ ₹₹

The open kitchen at Avo's serves traditional Goan flavours. Try the Cashew *feni* gelato.

8 Café Nu
MAP J1 ■ 182, Junos Vaddo, Pernem ■ 0985 065 8568 ■ ₹₹₹

Charming restaurant *(see p61)* located in a pretty garden offers light gourmet bites.

9 Tamil Table
MAP J4 ■ Socolvaddo, Assagao ■ 749 992 2517 ■ ₹₹₹

This beautiful courtyard restaurant is an excellent place to get a true taste of South India. It also offers innovative cocktails.

10 Thalassa
MAP H3 ■ Vaddy, Siolim ■ 0985 003 3537 ■ ₹₹₹

With outdoor tables shaded by palm trees, Thalassa *(see p60)* offers authentic Greek cuisine as well as picturesque views of the Arabian Sea.

See map on p88

TOP10 South Goa

Goa's idyllic south coast caters to a growing number of visitors every year. Fringed by some of the region's finest beaches such as Palolem, Agonda and Colva, South Goa's coastline is still more sedate when compared to the bustling beaches on the northern strip. Margao is the state's second city after Panaji, and is the main market town. The little hidden gem Bogmalo, once a quiet fishing village, is a perfect base for exploring the southern stretch. Inland, the villages of Chandor and Loutolim are scattered with a cluster of sumptuous Portuguese-era Goan mansions, including the delightful 300-year old Braganza House. Further east from Margao is Rachol, which is renowned as the site of a 16th-century Jewish seminary. In the far south, the Cotigao Wildlife Sanctuary is a paradise for birds and offers a rare glimpse of rich flora.

Bust at the Municipal Garden, Margao

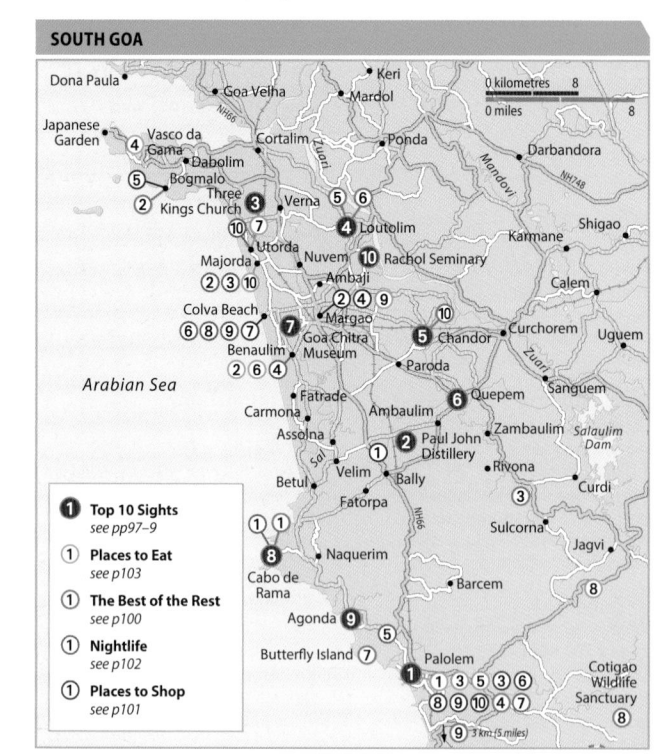

SOUTH GOA

- **1** Top 10 Sights
  see pp97–9
- **1** Places to Eat
  see p103
- **1** The Best of the Rest
  see p100
- **1** Nightlife
  see p102
- **1** Places to Shop
  see p101

Colourful wooden beach huts, Palolem

① Palolem
MAP D6

Palolem's *(see pp38–9)* beautiful bay is the busiest of the southern sweep of beaches but has lots to offer. It stretches for miles, and is lined with coconut palms, shacks and Thai-style camping huts. It also makes for a safe swimming spot for families. The restaurants are stylish and laid-back, serving a variety of international cuisines in addition to delicious Goan seafood and curries. You'll also find some places offering live music and DJs.

② Paul John Distillery
MAP D5 ■ M 21, Cuncolim Industrial Area, Cuncolim ■ 0744 778 8979 ■ Open 11am–4pm Mon–Sat

Goa is famous for its craft beers, gins and, now, India's first single malt, Paul John. You can take a tour of the distillery and visitor centre to undertand the unique process behind the creation of these drinks, visit the warehouses and, of course, sample its award-winning brew.

③ Three Kings Church
MAP C3 ■ Muder, Cansaulim

North of Cansaulim, perched atop a hill in Cuelim, is the picturesque Church of Our Lady of Remedios, commonly known as the Three Kings Church. It is believed to be haunted and harks back to the legend of three Portuguese kings, one of whom plotted to poison the others, but died himself in the process. All three were buried inside the church and ever since then, locals claim to have sighted ghostly apparitions here. The small church is famous for the Three Kings Feast *(see p68)* celebrated in January every year. During the feast, three young boys are chosen from any of the neighbouring villages to represent the three kings. The celebrations also include a colourful fair, which is held on the grounds of the church. Visitors can enjoy lovely views of the surrounding areas from here.

④ Loutolim
MAP B4

Picturesque Loutolim features several remnants of Goa's fine Portuguese heritage. In the heart of the village lies the majestic 16th-century Church of Salvador do Mundo (Saviour of the World). Nearby is Ancestral Goa *(see p35)*, which offers a unique glimpse into traditional trades and crafts from over a hundred years ago. The village is also home to many impressive stately homes, including the historic 500-year-old Figueiredo Mansion *(see p34)* and Casa Araujo Alvares.

Ancestral Goa in Loutolim

Antique furniture in the charming Braganza House, Chandor

Chandor
MAP D4

About 13 km (8 miles) east of Margao is the quaint village of Chandor. Between the 6th and 11th centuries, Chandor, then known as Chandrapur, was the capital of the Kadamba dynasty. It remained the capital until 1054 when the Kadambas moved to Govapuri, now known as Goa Velha (see p82). However, the Muslim invasion in 1312 forced the Kadambas to move back to Chandrapur, but only for a brief period as, soon after, the Portuguese invaded the city in 1327. Today, the main attraction in Chandor is Braganza House (see p100), which is regarded as the grandest of Goa's colonial mansions.

Palácio do Deão

This palatial mansion (see p35) is over 200 years old and was built by a Portuguese church dean. The unique architecture of this building is the result of a syncretic blend of Portuguese and Indian styles. The mansion, surrounded by lush gardens, is on the banks of the Kushavati River and offers spectacular views. Visitors can also enjoy a delicious Indo-Portuguese lunch on the terrace.

Goa Chitra Museum

With over 4,000 artifacts on display, this splendid ethnographic museum (see p35) is highly regarded by the Archaeological Survey of India (ASI). Founded by artist-turned-curator Victor Hugo Gomes, the museum showcases a unique collection of antique agricultural tools set up against the backdrop of a traditional organic farm. A unique aspect is its use of traditional recycling techniques. The museum is also home to the Goa Chakra museum, which displays ancient modes of transportation in India and Goa Cruti's collection, which features exhibits based on the state's colonial past.

Cabo de Rama

This picturesque bay in Canacona is a must-visit. The ruins of a medieval hillfort (see p39) occupy the coastline, providing the perfect backdrop for stunning views of the Arabian Sea. The fortress still bears signs of its tumultuous history, having switched hands between Hindu and Muslim rulers before being captured by British

---

THE VASCO SAPTAH

One of the biggest festivals in Goa, the Vasco Saptah has been a Goan tradition since 1898. It is said that during an epidemic, the locals visited the Zambaulim temple in Margao and brought back a coconut to Vasco. Soon after, a miracle occurred and the plague ended. The festival is now celebrated every year for seven days in August.

and Portuguese colonizers. There's also a small chapel near the fort. Along the cliffside, several hotels and restaurants have opened for tourists. The nearby Cabo de Rama Beach is a great place for a quiet stroll or a relaxing break from the bustle of Goa.

9 Agonda

With relatively few visitors, this pristine beach *(see p38)* makes for a great spot to sunbathe. The sea is slightly rough here, so the waters may not always be ideal for a swim. At the northern end of the beach is the nesting site of the protected Olive Ridley turtles. If you spot a turtle on the beach, do not disturb it or touch its eggs; there's a turtle rehabilitation centre here, which helps to conserve the eggs. Away from the beach, visitors can opt for yoga, meditation and Ayurveda classes.

10 Rachol Seminary

Built in 1606, the Rachol Seminary *(see p35)* is probably the most important of Goa's semi-naries. For generations, this was Goa's most prestigious educational institution, both for secular and religious studies. The entrance is covered with impressive murals and opens on to a central courtyard. The grand staircase, adorned with Hindu sculptures, leads to the library, which has a rare collection of Latin and Portuguese books. Attached to the seminary is the Church of St Ignatius Loyola, which has a beautiful 16th-century pipe-organ from Lisbon.

Façade of the Rachol Seminary

A DAY IN SOUTH GOA

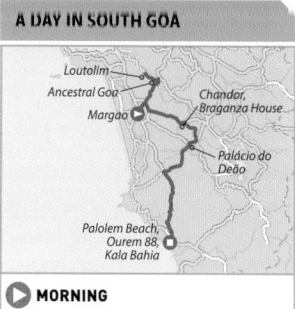

▶ MORNING

Spend the day admiring the iconic Goan architecture of the historic Portuguese-era mansions scattered inland from **Margao**. Head to the fascinating **Ancestral Goa** *(see p35)* in **Loutolim** *(see p97)*, also known as Big Foot Museum, a model village with life-size statues of craftsmen depicting early Goan village life. Next, drive 13 km (8 miles) east of Margao, to quiet **Chandor** to explore one of Goa's grandest colonial mansions, **Braganza House** *(see p34)*. The house built in the 1500s has a huge double storey façade with 28 windows flanking its entrance. A 30-minute drive southeast of Margao will lead you to Quepem, where you can stop for lunch at the superb **Palácio do Deão** *(see p35)*, a 200-year old Indo-Portuguese mansion. Enjoy a Goan meal on the terrace overlooking the river.

AFTERNOON

Next, head to **Palolem Beach** *(see p96)*, which is one of South Goa's most famous beaches. Lined with coconut palms, its clear waters are perfect for kayaking and stand-up paddle-boarding. Its gentle bay is great for children too. In the evening, head to **Ourem 88** *(see p103)* to have a sundowner followed by a sumptuous meal. Enjoy European gastro dishes made from fresh local ingredients. After dinner make your way to **Kala Bahia** *(see p102)* in Colomb, between Palolem and Patnem, for live music and electronic beats.

See map on p96 ←

The Best of the Rest

1 Cabo de Rama
This fort *(see p39)* belonged to various rulers until 1763, when it was occupied by the Portuguese. The observation post offers great views.

2 Naval Aviation Museum
MAP C3 ▪ Bogmalo Rd, Vasco da Gama ▪ Open 10am–5pm Tue–Sun ▪ Adm (additional charge for photography) ▪ www.navalaviation museumgoa.com
A unique military museum *(see p55)* which displays the evolution of the Indian Naval Aviation. It exhibits rare and old aircrafts and torpedoes.

3 Usgalimal Rock Carvings
MAP E5 ▪ Usgalimal Village
These petroglyphs *(see p39)* carved on laterite rock are one of the most important prehistoric sites in Western India.

Exotic Butterfly

4 Bliss Circus
MAP D6 ▪ Ourem Rd, Palolem ▪ www.blissaerial.com
Learn aerial skills or catch a contemporary circus show in the open-air amphitheater here.

5 Figueiredo Mansion
This 16th-century mansion *(see p34)* in Loutolim is older than the Taj Mahal. It is a fine combination of Indian and Portuguese architecture.

6 Ancestral Goa
Visit Ancestral Goa *(see p35)* to experience Goan rural life from the past century. It houses the Big Foot Museum as well as a mammoth sculpture of Mirabai *(see p55)*.

7 Butterfly Beach
North of Patnem and Palolem Beach lies the beautiful and uninhabited Butterfly Beach *(see p38)*, which is only accessible by boat. It is a great place to spot butterflies and dolphins.

8 Cotigao Wildlife Sanctuary
This scenic sanctuary *(see p39)* makes for a pleasant day-trip from Palolem. It is best visited between October and March.

9 Bamboo Yoga Retreat
MAP E6 ▪ Polem Beach, Loliem, Canacona ▪ www.bamboo-yoga-retreat.com
Considered a great space to practise yoga, Bamboo Yoga Retreat has three open-air, fully equipped, ocean-facing *shalas*, all with great views.

10 Braganza House
The biggest Portuguese mansion *(see p34)* of its kind, this 17th-century house is a unique example of Portuguese architecture.

Antique interiors of the charming Figueiredo Mansion

Places to Shop

1 Chitari's Traditional Art
MAP D5 ▪ 2499, Demani Wada, Cuncolim ▪ 0982 298 6793 ▪ Open 8:30am–noon, 2–6pm daily

Ask for directions from Cuncolim market to reach this workshop, known for its ornately painted and lacquered wooden carvings. Though the stock is limited, you may find *advolis* (cutting boards) or a *puja* (prayer) table or stool.

2 Margao Municipal Market
MAP B5 ▪ Open 9am–2pm & 4–8pm daily

The shops here sell a variety of items as well as Goan spices such as *trifala* or *teflam* (Sichuan spices) and *dagadful* (black stone flower).

3 India Love
MAP D6 ▪ Patnem Beach Rd, Patnem, Canacona ▪ www.indialovegoa.com

Vintage Indian textiles, upcycled denim with traditional patchwork and crafts from all over India are available at this beach boutique.

4 Tuk Tuk
MAP B5 ▪ 1st floor, Pereira Plaza, Margao ▪ 0904 901 7182 ▪ Open 10am–7pm Mon–Sat

With two stores, one in Margao and the other in Benaulim, Tuk Tuk is popular for souvenirs. Shop for quirky items such as handcrafted baskets, jewellery, clothes and trinkets here.

5 Zanskar Arts
MAP C3 ▪ Bogmalo Beach Rd ▪ 0832 253 8253 ▪ Open 9am–10pm daily

Find items ranging from pashminas and jewellery to gifts and trinkets here. You can also buy traditional souvenirs at this one-stop shop.

6 La Mangrove Boutique
MAP D6

Associated with a luxury resort of the same name, this bohemian-themed store offers beach- and lounge-wear.

7 Colva Beach Market
MAP A5

Attracting an international crowd, the Colva Beach Market offers a distinct and colourful shopping experience. Here you can shop for local items at negotiable prices.

Designer clothing at Chim

8 Chim
MAP D6 ▪ Palolem Beach Rd, Canacona ▪ 0832 264 3144 ▪ Open 9am–10pm daily

Set on the beach, this store has objects ranging from designer clothing to local craft items.

9 Jaali Boutique
MAP D6 ▪ Casa Jaali, Colomb ▪ 0800 771 2248 ▪ Open 9am–6pm Tue, Wed & Sun (until 10pm Thu–Sat)

Located in a shady tropical garden, this store sells typical Rajasthani jewellery as well as clothes, textiles and homewares.

10 Bunti
MAP D6 ▪ Palolem Main Rd ▪ 0706 629 3608

At Bunti, you can shop for sustainable, handcrafted fashion and homeware made in collaboration with Indian artisans. There's a good collection of kaftans and swimwear, as well as organic skincare products.

See map on p96

Nightlife

① Kala Bahia
MAP D6 ■ Colomb Bay, Canacona ■ 0976 635 0744 ■ Open 11am–midnight Wed–Mon

On the idyllic peninsula of Colomb Bay, this sunset bar, restaurant and lounge is perfect for a quiet, leisurely evening in South Goa.

Alfresco seating at Kala Bahia

② Edge
MAP A5 ■ 48/10 Alila Diwa Goa Village, Majorda ■ 0832 274 6800 ■ Open 9am–7pm daily

Setting the pace of the city's nightlife, Edge offers a unique experience. A pool bar by day, it transforms into a hip lounge in the evening.

③ Lorry Back Bar
MAP A5 ■ Vivenda Dos Palhaços Costa Vaddo, Majorda ■ 0832 322 1119 ■ www.vivendagoa. com

Located in a restored Portuguese house, this bar is actually a converted lorry. The painted back of the truck forms the bar's shutter. A nod to the Hayward family's heritage beer brand, this is an ideal place to enjoy a drink.

④ Adega Camoens
MAP A6 ■ Taj Exotica, Calwaddo ■ 0832 668 3333

Elegant black-and-white photos of Hollywood film celebrities adorn the line panels at this nightspot. The music enhances its old-world charm, making it perfect for a romantic evening over cocktails and cognac.

⑤ Leopard Valley
MAP D6 ■ Agonda Rd, Palolem ■ Open 10am–6pm Mon, Wed, Thu, Sat & Sun, 9pm–3am Tue & Fri ■ Closed mid-May–Oct ■ www.leopardvalley.com

This high-octane nightclub (see p57) is set in a jungle quarry. It features a 7-m (23-ft) high DJ stage.

⑥ Red Ginger
MAP A5 ■ Florida Garden, Colva Rd, Margao ■ 0888 847 6666 ■ Open 11am–11:30pm Mon & Thu–Sat (from noon Tue, Wed & Sun)

The stunning bar, great ambience and fabulous music makes this a great nightspot.

⑦ Neptune's Point
MAP D6 ■ Palolem Beach ■ 0915 843 2629

With a dreamy beach location, Neptune's Point is the place to groove to techno and trance beats.

⑧ Juju
MAP D4 ■ H.No 29/1, Gandaulim, Colva ■ 8956 691 430 ■ Open 12:30–3:30pm & 7–11:30pm daily ■ www.jujugoa.com

This modern Indian restaurant reimagines Indian dishes with a contemporary twist. Be sure to try the bartender's signature cocktails such as the tangy Karnatakila with tamarind or the Delhi 6 with jamun.

⑨ Club Margarita
MAP A5 ■ Colva Beach Rd, Colva ■ 0976 701 6858 ■ Open 8pm–2am daily

A popular hangout near Colva Beach, this welcoming place has a dance floor and offers good entertainment.

⑩ Jamming Goat
MAP D4 ■ Utorda, South Goa ■ 0937 343 1205

A friendly place with laidback beach vibes, Jamming Goat offers great cocktails, tapas and other small plates along with live music.

Places to Eat

PRICE CATEGORIES
For a meal for two, including taxes and service charge but not alcohol.

₹ under ₹1000   ₹₹ ₹1000–₹2000
₹₹₹ over ₹2000

1 Ourem 88
MAP D6 ■ South end of Palolem Beach, behind Rococo Pelton ■ 0869 882 7679 ■ Closed L ■ ₹₹₹

This quaint restaurant (see p61) has cosy interiors. Enjoy the music as you dig into the delicious food.

2 Leda Balcao
MAP A6 ■ Near Taj Exotica, Benaulim ■ 9607 074 710 ■ ₹₹

Savour the sizzlers and salmon as well as the Indian tandoori dishes that are offered here.

3 Zest Café
MAP D6 ■ Palolem Beach ■ 8806 607 919 ■ ₹₹

A beautiful beachfront restaurant serving delicious healthy fare. The raw desserts are a speciality.

4 Anantashram
MAP C3 ■ Father Jose Vaz Rd, Vasco da Gama ■ 0774 481 8888 ■ Closed Sun ■ ₹₹₹

Relish the traditional flavours at this local eatery. The Goan *thali* is delicious.

Striking interior of Anantashram

5 The Mill
MAP D6 ■ Dr Pundlik Gaitonde Rd, Palolem ■ 7517 683 611 ■ ₹₹

Set in a renovated rice mill this daytime café serves smoothies, great coffee and a good selection of brunch and lunch dishes.

6 Cavatina by Avinash Martins
MAP D4 ■ Bogmalo Beach, Vasco da Gama ■ 0832 278 9125 ■ ₹₹₹

The elegant Cavatina by renowned chef Avinash Martins is known for its Goan food with a modern twist.

7 Zeebop by the Sea
MAP D4 ■ Pereira Waddo, Utorda ■ 0832 275 5333 ■ ₹₹

Located right on the beach, Zeebop by the Sea has superb fresh seafood.

8 Mangaal Farmstay
MAP E5 ■ Mangaal Village, Quepem, South Goa ■ 7017 454 123 ■ ₹₹

This eco-friendly farm-to-table homestay (see p121) offers a unique communal dining experience. The food is prepared with organic, locally-sourced ingredients.

9 Longhuino's
MAP B5 ■ Ground floor, Dr Antonio Dias Building, Margao ■ 0832 273 9908 ■ ₹₹

Set in the heart of Margao, this place has maintained its vintage charm. The sausage and fish *thali* are favourites.

10 Spice Studio
MAP D4 ■ Alila Diwa Goa, Majorda ■ 0832 274 6800 ■ ₹₹₹

This menu at this award-winning restaurant celebrates the flavours of India's southwest coastal regions with a good selection of traditional dishes.

See map on p96 ←

Streetsmart

Colourful houses in Fontainhas,
Panaji's Latin-influenced old quarter

Getting Around

Arriving by Air

Goa International Airport, also known as Dabolim Airport, handles domestic as well as international flights. It is located 4 km (3 miles) from Vasco da Gama, 27 km (17 miles) from Panaji and 38 km (24 miles) from Calangute. Domestic flight carriers include **Air India**, **AirAsia India**, **IndiGo**, **GoAir**, **SpiceJet** and **Vistara**. There are also direct international flights to Goa from major hubs in the Middle East – Kuwait, Oman, Qatar, Dubai – and from London. Air India, **Air Arabia** and **Qatar Airways** are the international flight carriers.

The best option to travel into town from the airport is to take a pre-paid taxi. There are many pre-paid taxi kiosks outside the terminal, but prices may vary based on distance. Car rentals are also available.

Private and government buses offer a cheap means to transfer from the airport. However, they are unscheduled and infrequent, especially at night, and may not have space for bigger luggage – plan your route beforehand to avoid confusion. The scheduled AC-bus service to Panaji and Calangute is the more hassle-free option, though it has limi-ted frequency and does not operate at night. There are also local buses, which head to Vasco da Gama, outside the airport.

Manohar International Airport in Mopa, Pernem, a sustainable airport equipped with modern amenities, has also begun operations since January 2023. It is 19 km (12 miles) from Mapusa, 30 km (19 miles) from Calangute, 35 km (22 miles) from Panaji and 66 km (41 miles) from Dabolim Airport. It currently handles domestic flights to and from most major Indian cities; carriers include IndiGo, SpiceJet, Vistara and **Alaska Air**. International flights to and from London, Manchester and Moscow are also scheduled to begin operations in late 2023.

Pre-paid taxis and rental cars are available here as well. A special Blue Cab service, run exclusively by locals from the Pernem region, has also been introduced. This airport offers a scheduled bus service to Mapusa, Baga, Calangute, Panaji and Margao as well (check website for details). It is worth checking with your accommodation if it provides pickup or shuttle facilities from either airport.

Arriving by Train

There are two main railway stations in the southern part of Goa – in Margao and Vasco da Gama. You could also opt for a train that stops at Thivim railway station, which is closer to North Goa.

The Madgaon (Margao) station is the largest railway junction in Goa. It's the terminal for the semi-high-speed and fully air-conditioned Tejas Express and for the Konkan Railway, both of which run high-speed trains between Mumbai and Goa. The Tejas Express has two "vista-dome coaches" which have glass ceilings, large glass windows and rotatable seats – all of which allow passengers to enjoy superb views of the Western Ghats and the Konkan region. The coaches are also equipped with Wi-Fi connectivity and LCD TVs. A journey from Mumbai usually takes about 10 to 13 hours. An ambitious project, the Vande Bharat Express – scheduled to become operational in late 2023 – is expected to reduce this time to a mere eight hours.

The South Central Railway operates all its trains from the Vasco da Gama terminal. The Nizamuddin Goa Express (Delhi–Goa) also runs from this station, as do trains linking Karnataka. It is advisable to keep an eye on your baggage at the station.

You can book your train at the railway station or at the **Konkan Railway Reservation Office**, which is located at Kadamba Bus Stand. Tickets can also be booked online through the **Indian Railways Catering and Tourism Corporation (IRCTC)**. Check the **Indian Railways** website for train schedules, or call **Railway Enquiries** if you have any questions.

It is easy to travel to the city from the station as rail

terminals have kiosks for pre-paid taxis, as well as auto-rickshaw services.

Arriving by Sea

Mormugao Port Trust is Goa's main entry point for inter-state cruises. Set in Vasco da Gama, it is between the major ports of Mumbai and New Mangalore. It is 32 km (20 miles) south of Panaji, and can be reached by bus from Vasco da Gama station.

The two notable cruises that arrive at this port are the **Angriya** and **Cordelia** cruises, which sail on the Arabian Sea and ply between the ports of Mumbai, Goa, Chennai, Lakshadweep and Kochi. These luxury cruise liners provide all amenities, including accommodation, dining and entertainment.

Arriving by Road

There are two National Highways that lead into the state. NH 4, a well-maintained four-lane road, links Goa to Mumbai, Pune and Bengaluru, while NH 17 provides the shortest route from Mangalore. You can also take the NH 66 route from Mumbai to Goa. Mumbai, 587 km (365 miles) away, takes 11 hours to reach.

If you're travelling by car from Mumbai, the route via NH 66 features spectacular views of the Konkan coastline and rural landscapes along the entire route, including paddy fields and coconut plantations, especially during monsoon. There are meandering and steep roads on this route, which may not be the best option if you have car sickness. Be prepared to pay taxes at numerous toll booths along the way.

Driving and Traffic Rules

Carry an international driving licence if you plan on driving yourself. You also need to be well prepared for the traffic rules and road conditions in Goa. In India, driving is on the left and vehicles give way to the right. While driving on the highway, be careful of large vehicles, which often use muscle power to force you off the road. It is mandatory to wear a helmet if you are riding a two-wheeler, else you may be fined.

Speed limits range from 30 kmph (19 mph) to 60 kmph (37 mph). Drive slowly and look out for speed breakers especially at night, as the streets are poorly lit. The blood alcohol limit for drivers is 0.03%, which is equal to one drink. Seat belts are compulsory for drivers, as well as front- and rear-seat passengers; while this is not strictly enforced, it is extremely advisable for everybody in a car to use a seat belt. Avoid driving in the dark.

DIRECTORY

ARRIVING BY AIR

Air Arabia
📞 022 7100 4777
🌐 airarabia.com

AirAsia India
📞 1 804 666 2222
🌐 airasia.com

Air India
📞 1 800 180 1407
🌐 airindia.in

Alaska Air
📞 1 800 252 7522
🌐 alaskaair.com/

GoAir
📞 0922 322 2111
🌐 goair.in

Goa International Airport
📞 0832 254 0806

IndiGo
📞 0921 278 3838
🌐 goindigo.in

Manohar International Airport
📞 0832 249 9999
🌐 miagoaairport.com

Qatar Airways
📞 0793 061 6000
🌐 qatarairways.com

SpiceJet
📞 0987 180 3333
🌐 spicejet.com

Vistara
📞 0928 922 8888
🌐 airvistara.com

ARRIVING BY TRAIN

Indian Railways
🌐 indianrail.gov.in

Indian Railways Catering and Tourism Corporation (IRCTC)
🌐 irctc.co.in

Konkan Railway Reservation Office
MAP K6 ■ Kadamba Bus Stand, Panaji
📞 0960 462 9761

Railway Enquiries
📞 139
🌐 enquiry.indianrail.gov.in/ntes

ARRIVING BY SEA

Angriya
🌐 angriyacruises.com

Cordelia
🌐 cordeliacruises.com

Long Distance Bus Travel

Travelling by bus or coach means you often have a wider choice of timings, stops and itineraries; plus, buses can get to places that trains do not reach. It is advisable to travel by bus if you wish to save on expenses.

The state's main bus station is the **Kadamba Bus Stand**, which is 10 km (6 miles) from the Madgaon railway station. The **Mapusa Bus Stand** is a major transport hub for those visiting the beaches of North Goa. Keep in mind that bus drivers drive at high speeds, so be ready for a fairly bumpy ride. The **Karnataka State Road Transport Corporation (KSRTC)** and **Maharashtra State Road Transport Corporation (MSRTC)** offer regular bus services to Goa. A journey from Mumbai would take about 12 to 16 hours.

Bus fares vary depending on the route, distance and the type of bus that you are travelling in. Tickets don't need to be pre-booked for regular bus services, but bookings may be required for certain routes on deluxe buses; travellers can reserve tickets through travel agencies such as **redBus** and **MakeMyTrip**.

Domestic Trains

Goa has an efficient domestic rail network. Visit the IRCTC website for information on time-tables and tickets. It is better to use a local train in order to travel to far off places. For example, it is a good idea to take a train from Mapusa to Palolem, otherwise you will have to change between many buses.

Ferries

Boats and ferries are an age-old transport in Goa and are still an important means of commuting. Travelling by ferry is the fastest way to commute from the mainland to the islands. Cruises on the Mandovi – like the **Galaxia Galante** – offer lovely views of the city and its old buildings. Some also provide access to the backwaters of Goa, passing through Chorão and Divar islands.

Domestic Buses

The city has an extensive and well-connected bus network. There are two kinds of buses – the locals that halt at every stop, and the shuttles that travel to all the important sights. Buses from Panaji and Madgaon have easy connectivity to all the beaches in the north and even go to Ponda. Some private buses can be hailed, but the **Kadamba Transport Corporation (KTC)** buses can only be boarded at bus stops. The city's bus drivers are notorious for driving fast so be prepared for some hair-raising drives.

Buses run from 7am to 7pm and it might be difficult to find one beyond these hours. Tickets can be purchased from the bus conductor once you've boarded. Fares are affordable and range from ₹10–40, depending on the distance travelled.

Rentals

Hiring a car, motorbike or moped is one of the best ways to explore Goa, whether you're travelling solo or in a group. With rentals, visitors have the freedom of planning their trips without worrying about bus schedules or cab availability, both of which can be limited and erratic.

Car hire firms such as **Zoomcar** and **Super Car Rental in Goa** allow advance online bookings. Bike rentals are also available at every corner of Goa, particularly in Panaji. You could also ask your hotel or a local where to rent a bike from.

Drivers will need to submit their driving licence or any valid photo ID as collateral. Make sure to take back all documents from the dealer. Most rental agencies require drivers to be over the age of 21. For bikers, it is mandatory for the driver (but not the passenger) to wear a helmet – you should get one with the rental.

It is also important to test that the vehicle is in working order. It is wise to take pictures of the car or bike before renting it so that you aren't charged for any damage that you aren't responsible for.

Taxis

Before hailing or using a taxi, find out what the average fare for your journey is so that you can bargain accordingly. Relying on your accommodation to book a cab is a good idea; alternatively try either **Goa Cabs**, **GoanTaxi**, **Savaari**, **TaxiGo** or **TraveloCar** online, by phone, or via their apps. Cab availability fluctuates, especially at night and during festivals; renting a vehicle is a safer option.

Auto-Rickshaws

Auto-rickshaws or "autos" are the standard way of getting around Goa. They are fitted with meters, but most drivers won't use them and you will probably have to haggle. Know what price you should pay before stopping an auto, and agree to a fare before setting off. Fares should be ₹19 for the first kilometre then roughly ₹6.50 per kilometre. You can avoid having to haggle (and ensure you don't get overcharged) by hiring pre-paid autos at official set rates from kiosks at major transport terminals.

Motorcycle Rickshaws

Motorcycle rickshaws are the cheapest way to get around the city, with fares that can be negotiated. These vehicles are driven by drivers who are locally called "pilots". They can carry a single rider.

Walking and Cycling

Main roads and tourist spots in Goa can be quite crowded and noisy. However, its smaller roads and dirt tracks, lined with palm trees and surrounded by lush fields, are perfect for cycling or for morning and evening strolls. Take a stroll or cycle through the quiet villages of Assagao, Saligao and Chandor – dotted with brightly-painted colonial bungalows and pictur-esque churches – stopping occasionally for a cold beer or coconut water.

In the holiday season, residences are beautifully decorated with lights and festoons and make for a heartening sight in the evenings. Not all roads are well lit though – some can be quite deserted; sign boards are sparse and online map services can lead you down circuitous paths. It is advisable to not stray too far in the dark.

Fontainhas, Panaji's Latin Quarter, and Cabo de Rama are also popular scenic spots for walking and cycling, as are Chorão and Divar islands. Valpoi is popular among bikers and the bustling Mapusa Market also makes for an interesting walk.

Agencies like **Thrillophilia** offer guided walking tours around areas including the Dudhsagar Falls and the spice plantations in central Goa. Cycling tour packages are easily available online. E-bike tours, like those offered by **B:Live**, are becoming incredibly popular. Bicycle rentals are also available in the city.

DIRECTORY

LONG DISTANCE BUS TRAVEL

Kadamba Bus Stand
📞 0832 243 8256

Karnataka State Road Transport Corporation (KSRTC)
🌐 ksrtc.karnataka.gov.in

Maharashtra State Road Transport Corporation (MSRTC)
🌐 msrtc.maharashtra.gov.in

MakeMyTrip
🌐 makemytrip.com

Mapusa Bus Stand
📞 0832 223 2161

redBus
🌐 redbus.in

FERRIES

Galaxia Galante MAP L1 ■ Next to Maharajah Casino, Panaji

DOMESTIC BUSES

Kadamba Transport Corporation (KTC)
🌐 ktclgoa.com

RENTALS

Super Car Rental in Goa
🌐 supercarrentalingoa.co.in

Zoomcar
🌐 zoomcar.com/in/goa

TAXIS

Goa Cabs
📞 0986 012 2226
🌐 goacabs.com

GoanTaxi
📞 0986 085 5521
🌐 goantaxi.com

Savaari
📞 0904 545 0000
🌐 savaari.com

TaxiGo
📞 0832 671 1111
🌐 taxigo.co.in

TraveloCar
📞 0793 368 5555
🌐 travelocar.com

WALKING AND CYCLING

B:Live
🌐 tours.blive.co.in/collections/goa-tours

Thrillophilia
🌐 thrillophilia.com

Practical Information

Passports and Visas

For entry requirements, including visas, consult your nearest Indian embassy or check the **India Visa Online** website. Almost all nationalities (except citizens of Nepal and Bhutan) require a visa. Tourist visas are valid from 30 days to 5 years, depending on the type and e-Visa available for nationals of certain countries. For a longer stay, you'll need to apply in person or by post at the nearest Visa Office or alternatively at the Indian High Commission – there is a list of the latter on the website of the **Ministry of External Affairs** website.

Government Advice

Consult both your and the Indian government's advice before travelling. The **UK Foreign, Commonwealth & Development Office (FCDO)**, the **US State Department** and the **Australian Department of Foreign Affairs and Trade** offer the latest information on security, health and local regulations.

Customs Information

For laws relating to goods and currency taken in or out of India check the **Central Board of Indirect Taxes & Customs (CBIC)** website.

Insurance

We recommend that you take out a comprehensive insurance policy covering theft, loss of belongings, medical care, cancellations and delays, and read the small print carefully.

Health

Goa's heathcare system is good but quality in medical treatments will vary in public and private hospitals. Vaccinations against typhoid, tetanus, meningitis and hepatitis A are recommended. Make sure that you are covered against polio. Malaria and dengue fever outbreaks can occur, especially in and after the monsoon months (Jun–Sep); use high-DEET or PMD mosquito repellent.

Avoid food that is not freshly cooked, even unpeeled fruit unless you can clean it. In case of stomach upsets, drink plenty of fluids and stick to plain boiled food until the sickness subsides, or consult a doctor. **Manipal Health Systems Pvt Ltd** is one of the top research hospitals; other hospitals include the **Vintage Hospital & Medical Research Centre Pvt Ltd**, **Dr Kolwalkar's Galaxy Hospital** and the **Apollo Victor Hospital**. The **Wellness Forever** pharmacy in Panaji is open 24x7. For information regarding COVID-19 vaccination requirements, consult government advice.

Smoking, Alcohol and Drugs

Goa has numerous dry days. Smoking is banned in public places, and in places of worship. India produces hashish and marijuana bud, but both are illegal with harsh penalties in force for possession. *Bhang* (marijuana leaf) is legally sold in licensed shops in some places in Goa.

ID

There is no requirement to carry or show ID in Goa, and passports can usually be left in a hotel safe. It is nonetheless a good idea to keep a photo of your passport on your phone. You will need your passport to make train reservations.

Personal Security

Travelling in Goa is relatively safe, but it is recommended that you follow a few simple precautions. Wear a money belt under your shirt and be discreet with your camera and phone. While shopping, ensure shopkeepers make out a bill and process card transactions in front of you. Never accept food or drink from strangers, especially on public transport. Keep your baggage close at transport terminals and beware of staged distractions; padlock your luggage to the chain beneath your seat during train journeys. Contact your embassy if your passport has been stolen, or in the event of a serious crime or accident. There are also dedicated lines for the **ambulance, fire brigade** and **police**.

Although "eve-teasing" (sexual harassment) is a

punishable offence, women – both Indian and foreign – face unwanted male attention on a daily basis, and there have been incidents of rape and violence against female travellers. Do not completely trust cab drivers and tourist guides, and make sure to maintain a safe distance. Don't wander alone at night especially in rough parts of the state. Avoid walking alone in isolated places and in the rougher parts, or taking buses at night. When hiring a car or taxi, ask your hotel to book it for you (or go to a cab rank) and note the licence plate number. When queuing for train or cinema tickets, use the "ladies' lines", and the "ladies only" seats or compartments on buses and trains, if available. If you feel unsafe, please reach out to your nearest consulate or call the Tourist Helpline or the **Womens' Helpline**.

For the past few years laws banning homosexuality have been overturned as unconstitutional, but marriage equality is still under litigation. Hijras, who may be transgender or intersex, are semi-accepted as a third gender, but face much discrimination. Public displays of affection are seen as taboo for everyone. If you feel unsafe, call the helplines on **LGBTQ India Resource** for the nearest place of refuge.

Travellers with Specific Requirements

Goa can be challenging for the differently abled, but things are improving. The Dabolim airport and the new airport at Mopa are fully accessible to travellers with specific needs, with free transport provided in Kadamba buses as well as in ferries. Candolim Beach *(see p12)* is the very first wheelchair accessible beach in India. Boardwalks have been installed at the beach from the starting point right up to the water. There are wheelchairs with special tyres that are easy to steer on sand as well as those that float on water. Few restaurants are wheelchair accessible. Hotels are unlikely to have wheelchair-adapted rooms, and those that do will tend to be at the top of the market.

In April 2023, for the first time wheelchair-accessible e-rickshaw services have been introduced in the state. This will be managed by Ezy Mov, a pioneer in wheelchair taxi services. The service will be available from 7am to 10pm in Goa.

DIRECTORY

PASSPORTS AND VISAS

India Visa Online
🌐 indianvisaonline.gov.in

Ministry of External Affairs
🌐 mea.gov.in

GOVERNMENT ADVICE

Australian Department of Foreign Affairs and Trade
🌐 smartraveller.gov.au

UK Foreign, Commonwealth & Development Office (FCDO)
🌐 gov.uk/foreign-travel-advice

US State Department
🌐 travel.state.gov

CUSTOMS INFORMATION

Central Board of Indirect Taxes & Customs (CBIC)
🌐 cbic.gov.in/entities/

HEALTH

Apollo Victor Hospital
Station Malbhat, Margao
📞 0832 672 8888
🌐 victorhospital.com

Dr Kolwalkar's Galaxy Hospital
Duler, Mapusa
📞 0832 226 6666
🌐 galaxyhospitalgoa.com

Manipal Health Systems Pvt Ltd
Dona Paula, Panaji
📞 0832 300 2500
🌐 goa.manipalhospitals.com

Vintage Hospital & Medical Research Centre Pvt Ltd
Santa Inez, Panaji
📞 0832 564 4401

Wellness Forever
MG Rd, Panaji
📞 0832 242 4884
🌐 wellnessforever.in

PERSONAL SECURITY

Ambulance
📞 108

Fire Brigade
📞 0832 242 3101

LGBTQ India Resource
🌐 lgbtqindiaresource.in

Police
📞 100 or 1090

Tourist Helpline
📞 1 800 111 363

Women's Helpline
📞 1091

Time Zone

Goa is on Indian Standard Time (IST), which is 5.5 hours ahead of London, 9.5 hours ahead of New York, 12.5 hours ahead of Los Angeles, and 4.5 hours behind Sydney.

Money

The local currency is rupees (₹), which come in notes of ₹500, ₹200, ₹100, ₹50, ₹20, ₹10 and occasionally still ₹5, with coins of ₹20, ₹10, ₹5, ₹2 and ₹1. It is illegal to import or export Indian currency. If you have over US$10,000 in foreign currency, you must declare it.

Banks are usually open 10am to mid-afternoon Monday to Friday. Public banks are closed on second and fourth Saturdays of the month. Private bureaux de change are quite common, especially in Panaji and Calangute, and may offer decent rates. Mid- and upper-range hotels exchange foreign currency, but at poor rates. ATMs are common and accept foreign-issued credit and debit cards (especially Visa and MasterCard). These are widely accepted in upmarket shops and restaurants, but they may have an extra charge.

Electrical Appliances

The electricity supply is 220V AC. Most sockets are triple round-pin but take European-size double round-pin plugs. British, Irish and Australasian devices will only need an adaptor. North American devices will need an adaptor and a converter.

Mobile Phones and Wi-Fi

The country code for India is +91; the area code for Goa is 0832. If you are planning to use your mobile in Goa, check rates and accessibility with your service provider in your home country. SIM cards for mobile phones are widely available, but you will need your passport to buy one.

Most hotels and many bars, restaurants and cafés offer free Wi-Fi access.

Postal Services

There is a handy branch of the **Head Post Office** at Panaji. For poste restante, you will need to go to the **Arambol Post Office**. Packages need to be sealed.

Weather

It is best to visit Goa in winter (November–March). It can be extremely hot and humid from April to May (reaching 30°C/86°F), and rather wet from June until September, when the monsoon kicks in. The weather from November to March stays warm and sunny, with cool evenings. April to October are the months between peak and off-peak seasons when the beaches are quieter. Keep in mind that most of the restaurants might be closed during off season, and the seas are too rough for venturing out in boats.

Opening Hours

Shops typically open from 10am to 6pm Monday to Saturday. Many museums and some tourist sights are closed on Mondays. Popular malls such as **Mall De Goa, Caculo Mall** and **Big G** usually open from 10am. Shops and markets remain closed on national holidays.

The COVID-19 pandemic proved that situations can change suddenly. Always check before visiting attractions and hospitality venues for up-to-date hours and booking requirements.

Visitor Information

Tourist offices provide advice on sightseeing and detailed maps of the city, which can also be found in most bookshops. The **Goa Tourism Development Corporation (GTDC)** website has information and itineraries. Check for packages and events well in advance of your arrival. They also provide hotel bookings.

Local Customs

Eat with your right hand only, as the left hand is reserved for practical usages, like going to the toilet. It is customary to take off shoes (with the left hand) before entering a house. Putting feet up on furniture is considered bad manners, as is touching someone with your feet. If sitting on the floor, keep feet tucked underneath. Living in close quarters with family and neighbours gives Indians a different sense of "personal space" than many Westerners. If crowded or jostled, be tolerant as space is often at a premium. Indians tend to dress conservatively and keep the body well covered. Wearing shorts is not common, and women wearing clothes that display their legs, arms or stomachs will draw stares and unwanted male attention.

Language

Konkani and English are the official languages of the state of Goa. You will hear Konkani spoken everywhere, but almost everyone can speak English. Road signs are usually in English as well as in Konkani.

Visiting Places of Worship

It is best to dress modestly when visiting places of worship; wear trousers that are at least knee-length and avoid sleeveless tops (women should be covered from wrist to ankle). Remove shoes on entry to a temple, and if sitting, keep feet facing away from the main shrine. Photography is prohibited in some churches, temples and mosques so it's best to check on site before taking any pictures. Make sure to be respectful and accept any *prasad* (offering) with your right hand.

Taxes and Refunds

GST (Goods and Services Tax) is levied on all goods and services, typically at 18 per cent for nonessential items. It is included in displayed prices. While GST on souvenirs should be refundable to foreign

residents on leaving the country, no mechanism for this has yet been put in place.

Swimming

Due to the tropical weather Goa's seas have a pleasant temperature for swimming. Areas that are safe have been marked by red and yellow flags and life guards monitor beaches during strong currents and rip tides. During monsoons, stay away from the sea due to high tides. It is wise to swim during the day, and October to May is the best time.

Casinos

Goa is one of the few states in India where casino gambling has been legalized. The casino cruises that sail on the Mandovi are quite popular. Make sure you are aware of the gambling rules in casinos. Only those who are older than 21 years are allowed to enter the gaming areas. Casinos have stringent dress codes so wear semi-formal attire.

Accommodation

Goa has a wide range of accommodation options, from five-star hotels to mid-range budget and even backpacker lodges. You are likely to find a room to suit your budget wherever you go, but it is best to make reservations in advance. Rates for midrange accommodation are a bargain by Western standards. **Airbnb** is very useful for locating places to stay. **Couchsurfing**, which allows travellers to book stay with a family

for a short period, is also available in Goa. You could also book a room via the **OYO Rooms** mobile app as it offers good discounts.

Prices are likely to be higher during peak season, especially during Christmas and New Year. April to October are considered off-peak months. This is when you can find discounted hotel rates. Visitors should note that the government of India has imposed luxury taxes on hotels.

Places to Stay

PRICE CATEGORIES
For a standard, double room per night (with breakfast if included), taxes and extra charges.

₹ under ₹5,000 ₹₹ ₹5,000–10,000 ₹₹₹ over ₹10,000

Luxury Hotels

Alila Diwa
MAP A5 ■ 48/10, Adao Waddo, Majorda ■ 0832 274 6800 ■ www.alila hotels.com ■ ₹₹₹
Architecturally inspiring, this resort, close to Majorda Beach, overlooks the Arabian Sea. There are 153 spacious guest-rooms and suites and four great restaurants. Everything is state-of-the-art, down to the wood-lined loft rooms and 40 inch large plasma TVs. Indulge in Ayurvedic or Balinese spa treatments or lounge by the sea-facing infinity pool.

Caravela Beach Resort
MAP L2 ■ Varca Beach, Fatrade, Margao ■ 0832 669 5000 ■ www.caravela beachresortgoa.com ■ ₹₹₹
Set amid vast lawns, the classical Portuguese-style architecture of this resort blends its traditional charm with contemporary luxuries. Facilities include beach access, an outdoor pool, a golf course, and a variety of restaurants.

Goa Marriott Resort & Spa
MAP J6 ■ Miramar, Panaji ■ 0832 246 3333 ■ www. marriott.com ■ ₹₹₹
Offering sweeping views of the Arabian Sea, this resort is located in the heart of the city. Facilities include stylish restaurants, a swimming pool as well as a spa and fitness centre.

The Westin Goa
MAP H4 ■ Dmello Vaddo, Anjuna ■ 0832 663 6600 ■ www.marriot.com ■ ₹₹₹
This stylish hotel has comfortable rooms, some of which have forest or poolside views. It has a spa and a 24-hour gym, plus an outdoor pool and a kids' pool. There's also two restaurants, one of which is poolside. Despite its proximity to the vibrant nighlife of Anjuna, a stay here offers a calm and tranquil experience.

Grand Hyatt Goa
MAP C3 ■ P.O. Goa University, Bambolim ■ 0832 664 1234 ■ www. hyatt.com ■ ₹₹₹
With terracotta tiled roofs, beautiful courtyards and a swimming pool set among tropical gardens, Grand Hyatt Goa is unmatched in style and luxury. The hearty Sunday brunch is excellent.

The LaLiT Golf & Spa Resort Goa
MAP D6 ■ Raj Baga, Canacona ■ 0832 266 7777 ■ www.thelalit.com ■ ₹₹₹
A gorgeous lobby flanked by two grand staircases greets visitors at this hotel. Rooms are stylish with some overlooking the landscaped gardens and the nine-hole golf course. Watersport activities, sunset cruises, yoga and fishing are on offer.

The Leela Goa
MAP D5 ■ Mobor, Cavelossim ■ 0832 662 1234 ■ www.theleela. com ■ ₹₹₹
A landmark in Cavelossim, the Leela Goa has a secluded beach, freshwater lagoons and is known for its impeccable hospitality. The hotel boasts an award-winning spa, a golf course and a children's activity centre.

Taj Exotica Resort & Spa
MAP A6 ■ Calwaddo, Salcete, Benaulim ■ 0832 668 3333 ■ www.taj hotels.com ■ ₹₹₹
Set amid tropical gardens, the Taj Exotica exudes quiet elegance and luxury. Goan- and Portuguese-style rooms, with sea or garden views, have private verandas. The beachfront Lobster Shack offers excellent seafood, while Allegria is known for its traditional Goan cuisine.

Taj Holiday Village & Spa
MAP H6 ■ Sinquerim, Candolim ■ 0832 664 5858 ■ www.tajhotels. com ■ ₹₹₹
Set amid beautiful tropical gardens, this resort, close to Sinquerium Beach, has over 140 Portuguese-styled villas and suites. It features a swimming pool, a Thai restaurant and an Italian café.

Taj Vivanta

MAP L2 ■ St Anne's Junction, Dayanand Bandodkar Marg, Panaji ■ 0832 663 3636 ■ www. tajhotels.com ■ ₹₹₹

This Taj property is located in the heart of Panjim. With its fresh look and ambience, it appeals to the international traveller. The contemporary-style rooms are charming.

W Goa

MAP H4 ■ Vagator Beach ■ 0832 671 8888 ■ www. starwoodhotels.com ■ ₹₹₹

Tucked on a hillside above Vagator, W's flamboyant lobby leads to the Woo Bar, which has its own DJ console. The rooms are just as impressive, and come in categories, such as Wonderful, Fabulous and Spectacular. The Kitchen Table is an all-day diner, while the Spice Traders serves pan-Asian cuisine. There's also a Clarins spa on site.

Boutique and Heritage Hotels

Cavala Resort

MAP L2 ■ Calangute-Baga Rd, Baga ■ 0839 005 5518 ■ ₹₹

Dating back to 1979, the ivy-clad structure of Cavala immediately stands out. Goan architect Lucio Miranda designed this two-storeyed hotel with exposed laterite, tiled roof and balcãos (balconies) making it truly a vintage Goa property.

Coconut Creek Resort

MAP L2 ■ Bimmut Ward, Bogmalo ■ 0832 253 8090 ■ www.coconut creekgoa.com ■ ₹₹

Located on Bugmalo Beach, this tranquil resort is surrounded by lush palms and a meandering creek. It offers luxurious rooms with views of landscaped gardens. Facilities include a swimming pool, spa and a salon.

Vaayu Kula

MAP G2 ■ Junas Wadda, Mandrem ■ 9850 050 403 ■ www.vaayukula.com ■ ₹₹₹

Chic and intimate, this eco- friendly boutique resort is situated on the shores of serene Mandrem Beach. The rooms have a warm vibe with high wooden ceilings and offer stunning views of the Arabian Sea making this an excellent place to stay. There's a lovely beachside restaurant, a yoga space, an art gallery and a surf school.

Figueiredo Mansion

MAP B4 ■ Loutolim ■ 9552 017 514 ■ www. figueridohouse.com ■ ₹₹

This sprawling heritage property (see p34) has a unique old-world charm. Previously a museum, the hotel now features several rooms for overnight guests. It has six rooms with four-poster beds and beehive-tiled floors. There's also one family suite that can sleep four.

Lemon Tree Hotel Candolim

MAP L2 ■ Pinto Waddo, Candolim ■ 0832 248 9750 ■ www.lemontree hotels.com ■ ₹₹

Close to the Anjuna and Candolim beaches, this hotel is 5 km (3 miles) away from the 17th-century Fort Aquada. The rooms have contemporary designs, with balconies and access to a private pool. There is a vibrant café, terrace-top bar as well as a fitness centre on site.

Mateus

MAP K6 ■ 432 Rua 31 de Janeiro, Fontainhas, Panaji ■ 0744 748 8889 ■ www.mateusgoa.com ■ ₹₹

Set in a restored 1879 Portuguese mansion, this boutique hotel is conveniently located, close to the restaurants and waterfront in Fontainhas. It offers nine tastefully decorated rooms and has good service. Bike and car rentals are available.

Cabo Serai

MAP D5 ■ Canaguinim, Near Cabo de Rama Beach ■ 0788 788 2414 ■ www.caboserai.com ■ ₹₹

An award-winning eco-resort with spacious cottages and luxury tents overlooking the Arabian Sea. Facilities include a yoga space, a spa and a small pool. The resort is on a secluded hill above Cabo de Rama beach.

Panjim Inn & Panjim Pousada

MAP K6 ■ E-212, 31st January Rd, Fontainhas, Panaji ■ 0832 222 6523 ■ www.panjiminn.com ■ ₹₹

A 300-year-old town-house, now a heritage hotel, with period furniture. The adjacent three-storeyed wing overlooks the Mandovi, while the Pousada annexe across the road has two lovely rooms sharing a wooden balcony that overlooks a courtyard.

Island House Goa
MAP L5 ■ No. 45,
Piedade, Goltim, Divar
■ 0832 228 0605 ■ www.
islandhousegoa.com ■ ₹₹
A lovely Indo-Portuguese
house with comfortable
rooms, a bar, meditation
area, pool and duck pond.
From bird-watching to
fishing, there are plenty
of activities for guests
here. Goan dishes and
international fare is
served in the dining area,
which overlooks the pool
and garden.

Bate Papo
MAP J5 ■ Mudda Vaddo,
Saligao ■ 9243434318
■ ₹₹
A hidden gem in the
picturesque village of
Saligao, this boutique
homestay with rustic
poster beds has a relaxed
vibe. It offers delicious
Goan food. Pets are
also welcome.

Taj Holiday Village
Resort and Spa
MAP L2 ■ Sinquerim,
Candolim ■ 0832 664 5858
■ www.tajhotels.com ■ ₹₹
This elegant property
offers 39 luxurious rooms
and suites. The stunning
rooftop infinity pool offers
bird's eye views of the
surroundings and an
unparalleled swimming
experience. The night-
club, SinQ, makes it a
popular choice.

Amrapali – House
of Grace
MAP L2 ■ Morgado Vaddo,
Goa Velha ■ 93227 53726
■ www.amrapali-house
ofgrace.com ■ ₹₹
A gorgeous mansion set
in the heritage village of
Goa Velha, Amrapali is
situated on the banks of
the Zuari. It is a unique

boutique hotel with stylish
rooms and strives to
provide guests with a high
level of personalized
service. There's a great
courtyard pool and a
lovely café.

Vivenda Dos Palhacos
MAP A5 ■ Costa Vaddo,
Majorda ■ 0832 322 1119
■ www.vivendagoa.com
■ ₹₹
A mix of Indo-Portuguese
elegance and boutique
chic, this heritage
guesthouse occupies
a 100-year-old *palacio*.
Beautifully furnished
by owners Simon and
Charlotte Hayward, the
seven inviting rooms
have four-poster beds
and colonial furniture.
Interestingly, the rooms
are named after places
where the family has
stayed. Guests can enjoy
a drink at the Lorry Back
Bar *(see p102)*, which is
actually a converted lorry.

Aashyana Lakhanpal
MAP H5 ■ Escrivao Vaddo,
Candolim ■ 0832 248
9276 ■ www.aashyana
lakhanpal.com ■ ₹₹₹
Chic Aashyana Lakhanpal,
close to Candolim Beach,
has a stylish five-bed-
room villa, three secluded
casinhas (little houses)
and two Portuguese-style
bungalows, all tastefully
furnished. There's also a
fabulous diamond-shaped
pool and Ayurvedic spa.

Acron Waterfront
Resort
MAP L2 ■ Seaward side of
Baga Bridge, Baga ■ 0772
201 6888 ■ www.acron
waterfrontresortgoa.com
■ ₹₹₹
A part of the ITC Fortune
Hotel in Goa, this resort
extends across the Baga

peninsula. The rooms
provide modern amenities
in a rustic setting. In close
proximity to the beach
and the market, it is a
popular choice. There
is a spa and wellness
centre on site.

Ahilya by the Sea
MAP J6 ■ 787 Nerul-Reis
Margos Rd, Nerul ■ 0845
938 6478 ■ www.ahilya
bythesea.com ■ ₹₹₹
Overlooking Coco Beach,
Ahilya by the Sea features
charming Balinese-style
villas, which have seven
cosy rooms. The many
highlights of staying here
include the superb infinity
pool and a treehouse spa,
which offers massages.

Casa Palacio
Siolim House
MAP J3 ■ 62/1, opp. Wadi
Chapel, Siolim ■ 0982 258
4560 ■ www.siolimhouse.
com ■ ₹₹₹
An elegantly converted
350-year-old villa, which
was once the residence
of the governor of Macao.
Antique-furnished rooms
and suites are ranged
around a pillared court-
yard. Some have no air
conditioning or TV. Guests
can also stay next door at
the pretty, Little Siolim.

Casa Vagator
MAP H4 ■ H. No. 594/4,
Vozran, Vagator ■ 0703
091 3923 ■ www.casa
boutiquehotels.com
■ ₹₹₹
Smart and stylish Casa
Vagator offers deluxe
doubles and luxury
options, furnished with
sofas. Artworks and
handpicked artifacts
feature in all the rooms.
The terrace bar is a
great place to enjoy
sunset views. Next

door is the noisy Nine Bar, which plays trance beats from 4pm to midnight.

Elsewhere

For booking, email: gaze @aseascape.com ▪ www. aseascape.com ▪ ₹₹₹
Goa's best kept secret, the location of this beachfront property is only revealed if you are a registered guest. A collection of dreamy 19th-century villas, named the Piggery, Bakery, Priest's House and Captain's House, are separated from the mainland by a saltwater creek and can only be accessed via a bamboo footbridge. There are three creek-facing luxury tents too. A minimum one-week stay is required. Elsewhere remains closed from June to September.

Fort Tiracol Heritage Hotel

MAP G1 ▪ Pernem Taluka, Tiracol ▪ 0772 005 6799 ▪ www.forttiracol.in ▪ ₹₹₹
The seven luxurious rooms here are decorated in traditional Lusitanian ochre and white, with oxide floors, wrought-iron furniture and Indian textiles. The rooms have private balconies with sea views. The restaurant and lounge-bar (see p71) on the first floor offers authentic Goan food.

Nilaya Hermitage

MAP H4 ▪ Arpora, Bhati Bardez ▪ 0832 227 6793 ▪ www.nilaya.com ▪ ₹₹₹
Set on a hilltop retreat, Nilaya (or hidden dwelling) offers matchless views over the coastal plain. The rooms are beautiful and open onto a tiled pool. A *dhow* (teak sailing vessel) takes guests on cruises up the river.

Pousada Tauma

MAP H5 ▪ Porba Vaddo, Calangute ▪ 0976 580 4964 ▪ www.pousada-tauma.com ▪ ₹₹₹
This small, luxury resort has double-storey laterite villas ranged around a pool. Each has its own private dining area and patio, with a garden or terrace. The open-air Copper Bowl restaurant serves Goan food. A range of Ayurvedic treatments are available.

Rockheart Goa

MAP H5 ▪ 14 A/10 Annavaddo, Candolim ▪ 0981 932 7284 ▪ www.rockheart goa.com ▪ ₹₹₹
At Rockheart Goa, guests can enjoy the luxury villa experience created by legendary author Frank Simoes and his wife Gita. Close to Candolim Beach, this place has two lovely bedrooms and one guest cottage, all equipped with modern facilities.

Mid-Range Hotels

A's Holiday Beach Resort

MAP A5 ▪ Sunset Beach, Betalbatim ▪ 0982 238 1029 ▪ www.aholiday resort.com ▪ ₹₹
Stay at duplex villas, with private balconies that overlook the garden and beach. There is an outdoor swimming pool and a massage parlour too.

Mademoiselle Boutique Hotel & Café

MAP C2 ▪ Assagao, near Village Panchayat ▪ 91120 04853 ▪ ₹₹
On a quiet little street in Assagao, Mademoiselle is a stylish hotel with cosy

rooms, which each have an attached outdoor bathtub. It has a fun restaurant and a pool.

Granpa's Inn Hotel Bougainvillea

MAP H4 ▪ Gaunwadi, Anjuna–Mausa Rd, Anjuna ▪ 0866 965 6396 ▪ www. granpasinn.com ▪ ₹₹
Set amid lush gardens with a pool and terrace, is a 200-year-old Portuguese-styled mansion. There are three categories of rooms and suites; ancestral suites and standard rooms at the main house; and the poolside suites, with verandas and kitchenettes.

Palm Forest

MAP D6 ▪ Beind St Cruz Church, Palolem Beach ▪ 8007 727 269 ▪ www. palmforestpalolem.com ▪ ₹₹
The perfect blend of luxury and local Goan charm, this boutique resort has lovely rooms with pretty decor and spacious balconies. There's an ayurvedic massage spa. The resort also offers yoga classes.

La Cabana Beach & Spa

MAP G3 ▪ Ashvem Beach, Ashvem Wada, Mandrem ▪ 0982 283 5550 ▪ www.lacabana.in ▪ ₹₹
Stay in either the luxury tents, cosy cottages or villas at La Cabana. The air-conditioned tents have flat-screen TVs, minibars and sit-out areas. Some villas have sea views. Amenities include an outdoor pool and a beachfront restaurant. The spa offers treatments and therapies.

La Maison Fontainhas
MAP L2 ▪ 5/158, near
St Sebastian Chapel
Fontainhas, Panaji
▪ 0832 223 5555 ▪ ₹₹
Located in the atmos-
pheric Latin Quarter, this
cosy family-run heritage
home boasts beautiful
and elegant interiors.
Beautiful artworks line
the walls of the simple yet
chic rooms with en-suite
bathrooms. The European
Fusion restaurant, Desbue,
offers a creative menu.

Casa Jaali
MAP D6 ▪ Colomb,
Canacona ▪ 9309 591 796
▪ www.casajaali.com
▪ ₹₹
The accommodation at
Casa Jaali provides a
tranquil escape from
the bustling crowds of
Canacona. The huts and
beach house showcase
Goan architecture, with
tiled roofs, traditional
brick walls and locally
made furniture. It has
a great on-site café
and a shop.

Mojigao
MAP J4 ▪ Bairo Alto,
Assagao ▪ 7722081090
▪ www.mojigao.com ▪ ₹₹
Set in a beautiful tropical
garden with a spa and a
designated yoga space,
Mojigao is dotted with
lovely luxury huts. There
is a popular café, which
offers great Mediterranean
food, and sometimes
there's live music too.

Nanutel
MAP B5 ▪ Padre Miranda
Rd, opp. to Club Harmonia,
Margao ▪ 0832 672 2222
▪ www.nanuhotels.in ▪ ₹₹
Centrally located, this
three-star hotel is ideal
for business travellers.
Margao's bus and rail-

way station are 2 km
(1.2 miles) away. There
are 55 well-appointed
rooms and a multi-cuisine
restaurant next to the
pool. A travel desk helps
guests plan their
sightseeing itinerary.

Riva Beach Resort
MAP G2 ▪ Mandrem
Beach Rd, Pernem
▪ 0832 224 7612 ▪ www.
rivaresorts.com ▪ ₹₹
A casual riverfront
resort, Riva has riverfront
cottages and spacious
suites with sea views.
The multi-cuisine Buddha
Grill restaurant has a
coffee shop next door.
Ayurvedic treatments
are available at the spa.

Soul Vacation
MAP A5 ▪ 4th Ward,
Colva Beach, Colva
▪ 0832 278 8186 ▪ www.
soulvacation.in ▪ ₹₹
A short stroll away
from Colva Beach, this
concept spa resort has
comfortable rooms with
Mediterranean design,
which open out onto the
pool. The spa has an
in-house Ayurvedic spe-
cialist and the café has
indoor and oudoor seating.
Free Wi-Fi is available in
public areas only.

Budget Hotels

Alba Rooms Palolem
MAP L2 ▪ Palolem Beach
Rd, Palolem, Canacona
▪ 0992 356 9948 ▪ www.
albaroomspalolem.com
▪ ₹
Just 30 m (33 yards) away
from the beach's main
entrance, you will find a
green way to the lovely
garden of this hotel. The
rooms are clean and well-
lit, fully-equipped with
modern amenities. The

personalized attention
from owner, Sanjay,
makes the stay great.

The Banyan Soul
MAP H4 ▪ No. 962(1), off
Flea Market Rd, Anjuna
▪ 0982 070 7283 ▪ www.
thebanyansoul.com ▪ ₹
On the quiet southeastern
fringes of Anjuna, this
chic designer hotel has
attractively decorated
rooms, each with a pri-
vate outdoor sitting area.
Guests can relax in the
lounge area under an old
banyan tree. There's an
outdoor library here too.

Old Quarter Hostel
MAP M2 ▪ Fontainhas,
Panaji ▪ 7057 324 666
▪ www.thehostelcrowd.
com/oldquarterhostel ▪ ₹
In the heart of Panaji, this
hostel is ideal for those
who want to keep their
travel budget in check.
All dorms have bunk beds
with personal lockers.
There are also double
rooms with private bath-
rooms. The cost of
breakfast is included.

Martin's Comfort
MAP L2 ▪ Ranwaddo,
Betalbatim ▪ 0832 288
0765 ▪ www.martins
comfort.com ▪ ₹
This resort is managed
and owned by the same
people who run the
popular restaurant by the
same name. With its Goan
architecture and antique
furniture, this place gives
its visitors a glimpse of
Goan history.

Dreams Hostel
MAP H4 ▪ Vagator Beach
Rd, Coutinho Vaddo
▪ 9529 096 634 ▪ www.
dreamshostel.com ▪ ₹
A popular international
backpackers hostel

located in the heart of Vagator, Dreams Hostel is set in a restored Indo-Portuguese house. The hostel has dorms with or without air-conditioning, and even private rooms that fit the budget of every traveller. The amenities include a shared lounge, a garden with hammocks, secure lockers and free Wi-Fi. The in-house café serves all meals.

Oceanic
MAP D6 ■ Palolem-Patnem Beach Rd, Tembewado, Canacona ■ 0832 264 3059 ■ www. oceanicgoa.com ■ ₹
About a 10-minute walk inland from Palolem Beach, Oceanic's stylishly designed marble-floored rooms are fresh and relaxing. There is a pool on a forested patio as well as an excellent restaurant and bar.

Serene Waters Homestay
MAP L6 ■ H. No 130, Portais Chimbel, Ribandar ■ 9822488180 ■ ₹
One of the best homestays in Ribandar, Serene Waters provides scenic views of the pristine backwaters of Goa. Amenities include an infinity pool, a good restaurant and free Wi-Fi. This homestay welcomes couples so if you're travelling solo please enquire before booking.

ATS Goa
MAP B1 ■ Plot No. 697/3, Cliff Side, Sweet Water Lake Trek, Arambol ■ 070752 00000 ■ ₹
A short walk away from both Arambol Beach and Paliern Sweet Water Lake, ATS Goa is a good

option for travellers looking for affordable accommodation. It has clean, airy rooms with great views of the Arabian Sea. There's also a café on site.

Hotel Sun Inn
MAP D3 ■ Opp. Maruti Temple, Varkhandem, Ponda ■ 0832 231 8180 ■ www.hotelsuninn.com ■ ₹₹
A multi-storey business hotel, Hotel Sun Inn is a short distance away from Central Ponda. Choose from a range of deluxe, executive twin and pre-mium interconnected rooms here. An in-house restaurant serves good traditional Indian food.

Palm Grove Cottages
MAP A6 ■ House No. 1678, Tamdi Mati, Benaulim ■ 0832 277 0059 ■ www. palm grovegoa.com ■ ₹₹
Surrounded by pretty gardens, secluded Palm Grove is a 15-minute walk away from Benaulim Beach. All rooms have en-suite bathrooms, while some have private balconies. The deluxe rooms are in a separate Portuguese-style annexe. On site is an alfresco garden restaurant that serves excellent sea-food dishes. Some rooms have Wi-Fi.

B&Bs and Guesthouses

Wigwam
MAP H2 ■ Raj Villa, Dandoswada, Mandrem ■ 77694 10921 ■ www. wigwamgoa.com ■ ₹₹
There's a range of accommodation options

at Wigwam, a unique jungle resort in North Goa. There are luxury tepees, wooden cottages and a few two-bedroom apartments. It has a healing space and a popular café with pizza nights held every Tuesday. Bicycles and e-bikes are also available for hire.

Heaven Goa
MAP A6 ■ H. No. 104/3, Pedda, Sernabatim ■ 0832 277 2201 ■ www. heavengoa.in ■ ₹
This welcoming Swiss-run guesthouse has a dozen clean rooms, well set up with double beds, en-suite bathrooms and balconies.

Indian Kitchen
MAP H5 ■ 6/3A, Calangute–Baga Rd, Shiroli Pulachi, Calangute ■ 0832 227 7555 ■ www. indiankitchen-goa.com ■ ₹
Brightly patterned walls featuring mosaic tiling adorn the rooms of this guesthouse. Rooms range from basic to spacious apartments and wooden chalets, and are equipped with a fridge, a TV and a sit-out area. There is an extra charge for air-conditioned rooms and Wi-Fi. A pool and an Indian restaurant are on site.

Hospedaria Abrido de Botelho
MAP L2 ■ Rua De Natal, Fontainhas, Panaji ■ 0952 777 8884 ■ www. hadbgoa.com ■ ₹₹
This heritage hotel has large, tastefully decorated rooms with beautiful wooden and tiled floors. Breakfast is included and served in the rear garden.

For a key to hotel price categories see p114

Lar Amorosa
MAP J5 ▪ Chogm Rd,
Sangolda ▪ 7888047029
▪ www.laramorosa.com
▪ ₹₹
Lar Amorosa ("loving
home" in Portuguese)
is a boutique B&B housed
in an ancestral Indo-
Portuguese villa. Echoes
of the past are apparent
in the antique decor and
handcrafted furniture at
this upscale homestay.
There's also a small pool.

Lotus Sutra
MAP G2 ▪ Khalcha Wada,
Arambol Beach, Arambol
▪ 0914 609 6940 ▪ www.
lotussutragoa.com ▪ ₹₹
Some of these deluxe
air-conditioned wooden
cottages, have sea views,
and others offer garden
views. Rooms with
modern amenities and
balconies are available.
The restaurant and bar
has live music.

Michele's Garden Guesthouse & Café
MAP H4 ▪ H. No 955,
La Vie En Rose, Anjuna
▪ 0832 645 2601 ▪ www.
michelesgarden.business.
site ▪ ₹₹
In the heart of Anjuna,
this guesthouse has
four simple rooms, with
en-suite bathrooms and
balconies. The garden
café, La Vie En Rose is
open for breakfast only.

Beach Shacks

Chattai Beach Huts
MAP D6 ▪ Ourem, 81/5
Palolem Beach, Canacona
▪ 0877 964 8553 ▪ www.
chattai.co.in ▪ ₹
One of Palolem's more
stylish options, comprising
six well-spaced huts made
of *chattai* (straw mats)
right on the beach. All

have double beds and
attached bathrooms with
sit-out areas. Wi-Fi is
available in the restaurant
area only. Book in advance.

Dunes Holiday Village
MAP G2 ▪ Junas Waddo,
Mandrem ▪ 0832 224 7219
▪ www.dunesgoa.com ▪ ₹
The traditional bamboo
beach huts or tree houses
at Dunes have twin beds
and en-suite rooms equip-
ped with safety lockers. A
multi-cuisine restaurant
offers buffet and à la carte
meals. Free Wi-Fi.

Simrose
MAP D5 ▪ Near the St
Anne's Church, Agonda,
Canacona ▪ 75175 82394
▪ www.simrose-goa.com
▪ ₹₹
Conveniently located
close to Agonda Beach,
Simrose offers a wide
range of accommodations
to choose from depending
on your budget. Amenities
include a pool, massage
treatments and free
Wi-Fi. There's also an
excellent beachfront
restaurant serving great
food and cocktails.

Anahata Retreat
MAP G3 ▪ Ashvem Beach,
Mandrem ▪ 0832 259
0123 ▪ www.anahata
retreat.com ▪ ₹₹
Just north of La Plage
restaurant, this retreat
has 11 octagonal huts
made from dark mango
wood. Some are located
in the garden, others
on the beach and a few
have sea views. The
well-spaced huts have
verandas with good venti-
lation and quality beds.
There is a yoga space
and a good restaurant
as well as a lounge
area on the beach.

Ciaran's Camp
MAP D6 ▪ House No.
233/A, Palolem Beach
▪ 0832 264 3477 ▪ www.
ciarans.com ▪ ₹₹
A short distance away
from the beach, Ciaran's
features luxurious coir
and coconut-wood huts.
Some have roof-level
sundecks, daybeds to
laze on and to enjoy
sea views. On site is a
multi-cuisine restaurant
and a spa centre.

Palm Grove
MAP G3 ▪ Ashvem Beach
▪ 0965 706 3046 ▪ www.
palmgrovebeachresort.
com ▪ ₹₹
Set in a beautiful garden,
this chic place has six
bamboo huts, built from
sustainable materials.
Only one of these luxury
huts offers sea views.
There's also a two-tiered
beachfront restaurant.

Bamboo Yoga Retreat
MAP E6 ▪ Polem beach,
Loliem, Canacona ▪ 8381
047 343 ▪ www.bamboo-
yoga-retreat.com ▪ ₹₹
Learn and practise yoga
under the guidance of
expert teachers at this
Canacona resort. There
are three open-air, ocean-
facing yoga *shalas*, all
offering tranquil views
over Polem Beach.

Dwarka Eco Beach Resort
MAP D5 ▪ Cola Beach Rd,
Mattimol, Canacona, Cola
▪ 0982 337 7025 ▪ www.
dwarkagoa.com ▪ ₹₹₹
An idyllic beach resort
with ten paddy-thatch
cabins on the edge of
a freshwater lagoon,
which can be crossed
via a footbridge. The
simply furnished huts
with private bathrooms

feature a seating area, some have balconies. There is an outdoor swimming pool and bar. Free Wi-Fi is available.

Leela Cottages

MAP G3 ■ Morjim-Mandrem Rd, Ashvem Beach, Pernem ■ 0932 610 3486 ■ www.leela cottage.com ■ ₹₹₹
Stay in air-conditioned designer huts, just a stone's throw away from the beach. The interiors are furnished with antiques. A beachfront restaurant and rustic vegan café are on site.

Inland Retreats

Khaama Kethna

MAP D5 ■ 442 Gurawal, Agonda, Canacona ■ 0832 264 7958 ■ www.khaama kethna.com ■ ₹
A tranquil eco-village nestled on the hilltops of Agonda, Khaama Kethna features bamboo tree huts and five exclusive deluxe cabanas or lodges, with private terraces, which open onto lush gardens. All huts have outdoor bathrooms. There's a yoga and meditation centre and a garden restaurant.

Mangaal Farmstay

MAP E5 ■ Mangaal Village, Quepem, South Goa ■ 9422 464 264 ■ www.mangaalfarm stay.com ■ ₹₹
Surrounded by tropical gardens, the five-bedroom bungalow at Mangaal Farmstay offers a one-of-a-kind homestay experience. There are two deluxe rooms and three standard rooms. All have attached bathrooms. There's also a pool and a big communal dining

space. There is no TV or Wi-Fi access at the property. This homestay is about 8 km (5 miles) from the famous Netravali Wildlife Sanctuary.

The Inner Temple

MAP K4 ■ House No. 851, near Moira Club, Moira ■ 0950 357 7779 ■ www. theinnertemple.in ■ ₹₹₹
Set in the village of Moira, this gorgeous Portuguese villa has three beautifully designed large bedrooms, Kamini, Champa and Sachchidananda. All of these have calming interiors. There is a spa and private pool. In addition, yoga classes and meditation workshops are also organized.

Wildernest

MAP E1 ■ Off Sankhali, Chorla Ghat, Chorla ■ 0831 420 7954 ■ www. wildernest-goa.com ■ ₹₹₹
A self-styled eco-resort at an altitude of 816 m (2,677 ft), Wildernest has environmentally friendly thatched structures built with acacia wood and other local materials, but have the amenities of a luxury hotel. Guests can enjoy stunning vistas from the infinity pool. The resort has resident guides and organizes hiking and wildlife-spotting expeditions. Wi-Fi is available only in public areas. Minimum two-night stay required.

Hotels Around Goa

Evolve Back Hampi

Kamalapura – PK Halli Rd, Bellary, Hospet ■ 0839 429 4700 ■ www.evolve back.com ■ ₹₹₹
A short drive away from the ruins of Hampi,

this hotel is built to resemble a 14th-century Vijayanagara-era palace. There are 37 regal suites with opulent furnishings, and nine Jal Mahal pool villas. All have private Jacuzzis. The two restaurants offer gourmet continental and Indian cuisine. Amenities include an infinity pool, lounge bar and Ayurvedic spa. There are walking tours to help guests explore Hampi.

Hampi's Boulders

MAP G2 ■ Junas Waddo, Mandrem ■ 0832 224 7219 ■ www.dunesgoa. com ■ ₹₹₹
Along the banks of the Tungabhadra, this eco-resort is over an hour's drive away from Hampi. There are one to three bedroom boulder-shaped stone cottages, some with air conditioning, balconies and river views, but no Wi-Fi. Relax by the natural rock-cut pool and enjoy a South Indian buffet here. Walks and bird-watching tours are offered.

SwaSwara

Om Beach, Gokarna ■ 0956 259 1622 ■ www.cghearth.com ■ ₹₹₹
This tranquil beachfront resort is a short walk from Om Beach. It has relaxed open-sided wooden villas on a hillside overlooking the bay. All have en-suite bathrooms. A yoga hut and Ayurvedic centre are set in the gardens. Only the library has Wi-Fi. There are vegetarian and seafood restaurants. Boat cruises are also offered. Minimum five-night stay.

For a key to hotel price categories see p114

General Index

Acknowledgments

This edition updated by

Contributor Victoria McCulloch
Senior Art Editor Stuti Tiwari
Project Editor Anuroop Sanwalia
Editor Mark Silas
Assistant Editor Nandini Desiraju
Picture Research Administrator Vagisha Pushp
Picture Research Manager Taiyaba Khatoon
Publishing Assistant Simona Velikova
Jacket Designer Jordan Lambley
Senior Cartographer Subhashree Bharati
Cartography Manager Suresh Kumar
DTP Designer Rohit Rojal
Senior Production Editor Jason Little
Senior Production Controller Kariss Ainsworth
Managing Editors Shikha Kulkarni, Beverly Smart, Hollie Teague
Managing Art Editor Sarah Snelling
Senior Managing Art Editor Priyanka Thakur
Art Director Maxine Pedliham
Publishing Director Georgina Dee

DK would like to thank the following for their contribution to the previous editions: Beverly Smart, Meenakshi Sharma

The publisher would like to thank the following for their kind permission to reproduce their photographs:

Key: a-above; b-below/bottom; c-centre; f-far; l-left; r-right; t-top

123RF.com: espies 59br.

Alamy Stock Photo: Ian Dagnall 100b; Dinodia Photos 3tl, 45br, 72–3, 99bl; Exotica 74tl, 97br; Hemis.fr / Soularue 95tl; Indigo Photos 48b; Filip Jedraszak 54b; Andrey Khrobostov 89bl; Nikreates 96cla; Simon Reddy 98t, 104–5.

Anantashram: 103bl.

Ashiyana Yoga Retreat Village: 18clb.

Baba Au Rhum: 61cl.

The Black Sheep Bistro: 79c.

Bomras: 60bl.

Butterfly Conservatory of Goa: 100c.

Sangram Chatterjee: 11tr, 12bl, 13tl, 13crb, 16–7c, 17tl, 20cl, 21crb, 22crb, 27cl, 44tl.

Chim, Goa: 101tr.

Club Titos: 94b.

Dorling Kindersley: Fredrik Arvidsson / Laurence Arvidsson 42t, 42bc.

Dreamstime.com: Aapthamithra 4crb, 70–1b; Allenkayaa 6cla, 11cla, 30br; Alukashenkov 83cla; Andrey64 18br; Sibi Ar 39clb; Swapan Banik 10cla, 16br; Florian Blümm 15tr, 66t; Boggy 26br; Natalia Bogutckaia 24cla; Andrei Bortnikau 18-9c; Paul Brighton 58br; Bubbawillums 97tl; Adrian Constantinescu 67tr; Viktoriya Samir Dixit 70tl; Stefano Ember 12-3c; Euriico 22t; Francocogoli 85c; Girishhc 32bl, 84cla; Denys Hedrovych 7tr; Valerii Iavtushenko 14–5b, 71cr; Jackmalipan 23bl; Joviton 4b, 68cl, 69br; Maxim Karlione 38–9b; Milind Ketkar 2tr, 40–1; Konstik 33tl; Kosmos111 11b, 64–5; Iuliia Kryzhevska 10bl; Manubahuguna 58cl, 59tl; Jose Mathew 15cl, 34cl, 38cr, 39tr, 50–1bc, 69tl, 93tl; Aliaksandr Mazurkevich 77cl; Alexander Mychko 59clb; Vishnu Nair 32cr; Kantilal Patel 4cl, 51tr; Marina Pissarova 3tr, 4t, 4cla, 19tl; Ondřej Prosický 11cra; Radiokafka 45t, 68b, 75tr; Dmitry Rukhlenko 47t; Saiko3p 10cl, 10crb, 14cla, 20–1c, 24–5b, 30–1c, 47t, 62tl, 81br, 89t; Snehal Jeevan Pailkar 27b; Peppy Graphics 50cl; Nataliia Sokolovska 24crb, 26tl, 36ca, 36b, 37crb; Spwkr 10tr, 28–9; Evgenii Sudarev 4clb; Suronin 4cra; Aleksandar Todorovic 2tl, 8–9, 11cr, 47br; Lloyd Vas 51tl; Victortyakht 55c; Alex Zarubin 25tl; Oleg Zhukov 31tr, 80cl.

Gallery Gitanjali: 20br.

Getty Images: Lonely Planet Images / Greg Elms 91cl; Moment / Ashit Desai 86–7; Stone / Jon Hicks 1.

Goa Chitra Museum: 34br.

Deveshi Halder: 76t.

Getty Images / iStock: 1970s 81t; Pavel Laputskov 46cl; Pavel Sipachev 52–53; VasukiRao 84br.

Jungle Book: 33crb.

Kala Bahia: 102cla.

Murugaya xpedition: 49tl.

Nilesh Korgaokar: 34–5c, 82b.

Literati: 17br.

LPK Waterfront: 57b.

Mario Gallery: 67bl, 78b.

Museum Houses of Goa: 90b.

Museum of Goa: 43tr, 88tl, 90tl.

Paper Boat Collective: 62br, 93br.

People Tree: 63tl.

Photo Division Ministry of Information and Broadcasting: 43cl.

Prana Café: 61bc.

Satsanga Retreat: 92clb.

Serendipity Art Festival: St+Art India Foundation / Mural by Okuda 66cl.

Shishir Dhulla: @chitrakatha.in 35crb.

Sinq Night Club: 56t.

Mehak Singhal: 31cr.

Soul Travelling- Mud Bath, Charao: 48tl.

Sublime - Goa: 60t.

Sunaparanta, Goa: 23tr, 37tl.

Velha Goa: 63br.

Brian Yardley: 55tr.

Cover images

Front and spine: **Getty Images:** Stone / Jon Hicks.

Back: **AWL Images:** GARDEL Bertrand tr; **Dreamstime.com:** Mcherevan tl, Spvvkr cla; **Getty Images:** Stone / Jon Hicks b; **Getty Images / iStock:** alan64 crb.

Pull Out Map Cover

Getty Images: Stone / Jon Hicks.

All other images © Dorling Kindersley
For further information see:
www.dkimages.com

First edition 2019

Published in Great Britain by
Dorling Kindersley Limited
DK, One Embassy Gardens, 8 Viaduct
Gardens, London SW11 7BW, UK

The authorised representative in the EEA is
Dorling Kindersley Verlag GmbH. Arnulfstr.
124, 80636 Munich, Germany

Published in the United States by
DK Publishing, 1745 Broadway, 20th Floor,
New York, NY 10019, USA

A CIP catalogue record is available
from the British Library.

A catalogue record for this book is available
from the Library of Congress.

ISSN 1479-344X
ISBN 978-0-2416-2504-0

Printed and bound in Malaysia

www.dk.com

As a guide to abbreviations in visitor information blocks: **Adm** = *admission charge;* **D** = *dinner;* **L** = *lunch.*

MIX
Paper | Supporting
responsible forestry
FSC™ C018179

This book was made with Forest
Stewardship Council™ certified
paper – one small step in DK's
commitment to a sustainable future.
**For more information go to
www.dk.com/our-green-pledge**